About the Author

Anthony Le Donne (PhD, Durham) is Assistant Professor of New Testament at United Theological Seminary. He is the author/editor of seven books and serves as an editor of the *Journal for the Study of the Historical Jesus*.

THE WIFE
OF JESUS

ANCIENT TEXTS AND
MODERN SCANDALS

ANTHONY
LE DONNE

ONEWORLD

A Oneworld Book

First published by Oneworld Publications, 2013

This paperback edition published by Oneworld Publications, 2015

Copyright © Anthony Le Donne 2013

The moral right of Anthony Le Donne to be identified as
the Author of this work has been asserted by him in accordance
with the Copyright, Designs, and Patents Act 1988.

All quotations from Jewish and Christian Scriptures are
taken from the New Revised Standard Version of
the Bible unless otherwise noted.

ISBN 978-1-78074-569-5
eISBN 978-1-78074-306-6

Printed and bound in Great Britain by Clays Ltd, St Ives plc

Oneworld Publications
10 Bloomsbury Street
London
WC1B 3SR
United Kingdom

Stay up to date with the latest books,
special offers, and exclusive content from
Oneworld with our monthly newsletter

Sign up on our website
www.oneworld-publications.com

To my siblings:
Lisa, Lara, Amber, Tim, and Tara

Contents

	List of Illustrations	viii
	Foreword	ix
	Acknowledgments	xiii
	Introduction: The Quest(ion) of the Wife of Jesus	1
1	According to the Flesh	9
2	Substance and Shadow	25
3	Something about Mary	40
4	Mrs. Christ	53
5	Smithing Jesus	69
6	From Persia, with Love	91
7	Average Joe	106
8	Alternative Lifestyle	118
9	Bride of Christ	130
10	Was Jesus Married?	147
	Afterword: Portraits and Mirrors	163
	Notes	167
	Bibliography	191
	References Index	200
	Subject Index	204

LIST OF ILLUSTRATIONS

p. 13 Rembrandt van Rijn, *Christ on the Cross*, 1631[*]

p. 31 Rembrandt van Rijn, *Healing of Peter's Mother-in-Law*, *c*. 1660[*]

p. 48 Quinten Matsys, *Saint Mary Magdalene*, *c*. 1520[*]

p. 63 *The Gospel of Jesus' Wife*[*]

p. 70 Michelangelo, *Crucifixion*, *c*. 1541[*]

p. 71 Warner Sallman, *Head of Christ*, *c*. 1940

p. 73 "A Mormon and his wives dancing to the devil's tune", *c*. 1850

p. 87 Photograph of Mar Saba, *c*. 1895[*]

p. 95 *Layla and Majnun*, *c*. 18th century[*]

p. 136 Jan van Eyck, *The Ghent Altarpiece: Adoration of the Mystic Lamb*, *c*. 1425[*]

p. 149 artist unknown, *Nursing Madonna*, *c*. 16th century[*]

[*]Sourced via Wikimedia Commons

FOREWORD

In December 2012, the University of the Pacific invited me to speak at a public forum based on this question: *Did Jesus have a wife?* The panel of experts came to fairly conservative conclusions. The Coptic expert, a scholar of early Christianity, suggested that the recently publicized "Gospel of Jesus' Wife" might be a modern forgery. The religious ethics professor suggested that religiously minded folks shouldn't be scandalized by (what should be) an uncontroversial question. After all, no less than the Chalcedonian creed (composed in 451 and accepted as doctrine by Eastern Orthodox, Catholic and many Protestant Christian churches) stated that Jesus was "fully human, like us in all respects, apart from sin." The expert on ancient Judaism reminded us that the ancients were less scandalized by sex than we are. I spoke on the topic from the perspective of a professional historian.

I talked about marriage practices during Jesus' time and suggested that Jesus might have been married in his young adulthood. I then offered several reasons why Jesus might not have been the "marrying type." All in all, I was grateful to have been involved in a thoroughly sane and open exchange. Unlike recent treatments of this topic in film, documentary, and novel, none of the scholars at this forum were conspiracy theorists. There were no theories forwarded about Jesus and Mary Magdalene or their secret descendants. No one used the occasion to promote a scandal of any kind.

Yet in the weeks leading up to this event, the question itself became fodder for several newspaper blogs around the Stockton, California area. In response to some local publicity about the forum, several social media outlets channeled an outburst of hostility. The question *Did Jesus have a wife?* was immediately threatening before any answers had been given.

One blog commenter accused the university of having a secret agenda to "attack the Christian religion." This same commenter claimed that "secular organizations never miss an opportunity to ridicule and mock people [who] claim to be Christian." On a different website, a letter to the editor was published claiming that our forum was "speculating on God's sex life." Another commenter simply wrote: "I think it is nonsense." Again, these reactions were published *before* the forum took place! It seems that the question itself, let alone any attempts to answer it, is cause for great controversy and hostility.

I was anticipating, given this initial reaction, that the event itself would be a bit hairy. But, to my surprise and relief, all in attendance were civil and hospitable. None of the ivory-tower scholars howled at the moon, and the townspeople left their pitchforks and torches at home. What I learned from this experience is that the topic of "the wife of Jesus" brings a host of expectations with it. This topic has been sold as a scandal for so long that people can't help but be scandalized by it. But – and this was the most intriguing aspect for me – people tend to be more scandalized by the question itself and less so by the answers. I have found this to be true even when the answers are a bit unexpected and unsettling.

These were the early steps of an unexpected journey. While I have dedicated my life to historical Jesus research (so I am *anything but* impartial), I really had no idea what I would discover on my quest for the wife of Jesus. I had no predetermined conclusions; I only knew that the topic was worth exploring. Indeed, any topic that enrages and fascinates so many people is important – if for no other reason than to tell us something about ourselves. In addition, the fact that so few professional historians are willing to engage with the topic is intriguing.

At times my conclusions surprised me; at times the Jesus I discovered was troubling. More often than I would have hoped, I had to conclude with better questions rather than definitive answers. Sometimes I was compelled to draw an uncomfortable conclusion. The process of writing this book kept me guessing until the very end. I hope that you enjoy the journey in the reading as much as I did in the writing.

Anthony Le Donne
Sebastopol, California

ACKNOWLEDGMENTS

I would like to thank the University of the Pacific for their invitation to lecture on the topic related to this book. It was the fruitful discussions I had with the fine attendees in Stockton, CA that planted the seeds first. My thanks to Larry Behrendt, Chad T. Carmichael, Bruce Chilton, April DeConick, Mark Goodacre, Stephanie Barbé Hammer, Joel Kaminsky, Chris Keith, Anne Lapidus Lerner, Joel N. Lohr, Dan Melligan, Christopher W. Skinner, Caroline T. Schroeder, Eric Thurman, and John G. Turner who graciously read portions of the book and made helpful suggestions for improvement. I also extend my gratitude to Ovidiu Creangă for providing me with an early draft of his forthcoming book. Any deficiencies that remain belong to me alone.

I'm also deeply grateful for the beautiful and discerning eyes of my wife Sarah. Her willingness to fight for the aesthetics of grammar and against the evils of over-hyphenation has made me a better communicator. Finally, I want to thank my five siblings, to whom this book is dedicated. They have been the best Arab, French, African-American, Italians that anyone could ask over for Sunday lunch.

Introduction

THE QUEST(ION) OF
THE WIFE OF JESUS

It is a Quest and not a Conquest.
– DAGMAR WINTER

Before Jesus rode into Jerusalem, before his clever stories gave way to righteous indignation, before he marched hell-bent toward fate, he was just another overzealous, drawling preacher from up north. At least, this is how he would have seemed to the people of Jerusalem. Indeed, before his crew of castoffs entered the city, few people in Jerusalem knew much about him. Chances are that they'd never heard of him before. But Jesus would soon draw quite a crowd. Jesus preached politics and accused religious luminaries of corruption. There were rumors of faith healings, demons, and revolution . . . *and who were all of these women with him?*

Those who wondered who he was and what he stood for wanted to know, "By what authority are you doing these things?" Witty to the last, Jesus replied with a question of his own. He asked about the famous John the Baptist: was John's authority endorsed by God, or not? In other words, Jesus was asking, "Was John a prophet or a fake?" The leaders of Jerusalem knew better than to disparage the recently executed Baptizer. John, it seems, was the famous one. Long before Jesus was making outlandish claims in the holiest place on Earth, he was just riding the camel-haired coattails of John the Baptist.

So this is how Jesus introduced himself to the leaders of Jerusalem. This is how the biblical Gospels introduce Jesus as well. Matthew, Mark, Luke, and John – all begin their stories of Jesus with an endorsement from John. A great many historical Jesus scholars argue that John was Jesus' mentor. And so I begin this book in the same way. Whatever their relationship, these two prophets had enormous respect for one another.

Jesus and John had a great deal in common. If we look to their portraits in the New Testament, both preached repentance and about the politics of God. Both were rumored to be the messiah of Israel. Luke's Gospel even claims that they were cousins. In fact, one of the only noticeable differences between Jesus and John concerned carnality.

It seems that John was against creature comforts; he shunned fine clothing, avoided feasts, ate sparingly, and refused wine. Most scholars believe that John chose an "ascetic" lifestyle. Asceticism is the belief that a new and better self can emerge when a person withdraws from normal life. Ascetics often deprived themselves of worldly comforts and pleasures such as fine clothing, food, wine, sex, marriage, family, and so on.

This is where the topic of John the Baptist gets interesting. Did he, as we would expect from an ascetic, choose a life of celibacy? We don't know if the Baptist was celibate, but he does seem to fit the profile. After all, he had withdrawn from society. He lived in the wilderness and foraged food from bees and bugs.

The vast majority of Jewish men, especially religious leaders, were married. There are very few examples of celibate Jewish men in the first century. The few Jewish men who did choose celibacy in the first century were ascetics. One could say that asceticism and celibacy fit hand-in-glove.[1]

John's general lifestyle seems to be that of an ascetic and this, in all likelihood, would have included celibacy. And so this is the stance that many historians have taken: John was probably the rare example of a single, Jewish religious leader.

Jesus, on the other hand, was not an ascetic. New Testament scholar Dale B. Martin lists examples of Jewish asceticism that might have included celibacy in or near the first century. Noticing that these examples tend to show extreme concerns for purity of worship, abstinence from feasts and wine, and/or a general retreat from society, he writes that "we now know of several forms of Jewish asceticism current in Jesus' day. But Jesus fits none of them."[2]

More to this point, Jesus allowed patrons to support his ministry. Luke's Gospel tells us that wealthy women supported Jesus and that he accepted their hospitality. The end of Mark's Gospel reveals that several of these women traveled with Jesus. Mary Magdalene and a woman named "Salome" were included among Jesus' traveling companions. The *Gospel of Thomas* claims that Jesus accepted Salome's hospitality, including food and a comfortable place to recline and discuss discipleship while he ate. John the Baptist, by every indication we have, did not accept such comforts. Indeed, John's retreat from social normalcy was so extreme that he was demonized. Luke's Gospel includes this saying from Jesus: "For John the Baptist has come eating no bread and drinking no wine; and you say, 'He has a demon.' The Son of man has come eating and drinking; and you say, 'Behold, a glutton and a drunkard, a friend of tax collectors and sinners!' Yet wisdom is justified by all her children."[3]

While they had a great deal in common, the one noticeable difference was that Jesus (as compared to John) gained a reputation for hedonism. Jesus accepted patronage, befriended wealthy and generous people, attended their feasts, drank their wine, and – yes – he brought women with him. It is, then, no mystery as to why Jesus gained the reputation of a "glutton and a drunkard." By almost every indication, Jesus was the mirror opposite to John's asceticism.

John, we think, chose celibacy for ascetic reasons.

Did Jesus?

THE FORGE OF CULTURE

A large portion of this book will offer arguments for and against a possible wife of Jesus. I will also explore various (ancient and modern) attempts to project sexual ethics onto Jesus. As our most celebrated and despised cultural icon, Jesus is always being remade to suit various social norms. That is what this book is about. The title "Wife of Jesus" suggests two things to me. First, it indicates a quest for an answer to the question "Was Jesus married?" Second, it indicates a cultural construct of the modern Christianized West. In this second sense, this book is about a topic that reveals our simultaneous fascination with and repulsion of the idea that Jesus might have been married.

Historians, when the topic relates to Jesus, tarry on that perilous border between the traditional icon and the ever-emerging iconoclast. Our various Jesuses are employed to lobby for our agendas. This has been most recognizable in recent years as debates over sex, gender, and family have come to center stage in the Christianized West. We who live in the wake of Christendom have leveraged Jesus' legacy for a variety of causes and reasons.

For better or worse, we will continue to project our sexual norms and aspirations for progress onto the historical Jesus. Jesus will not remain silent on the subjects of sex, gender, and family. He won't remain silent because the Christianized West will not afford him that right. Jesus lobbies on both sides. The recognition of this dynamic, coupled with our ongoing fascination with Jesus' marital status, motivated me to write this book.

The wife of Jesus is a topic that ancient Christians explored and the Christianized West continues to explore, often haphazardly. Both ancient and recent controversies about the wife of Jesus reflect cultural obsessions and sexual taboos. So, in many ways, this book is an exploration of the evolving sexual identity of the Christianized West. But it is also about Jesus and the possibility that he was married.

There is perhaps no historical topic so fascinating to the general public that is so seldom addressed by professional historians. Fictions, films, and forgeries continue to raise our collective hope for some indication that Jesus was married. A predictable media swell now finds a pressure valve once every four or five years. All the while voices from the ivory tower tell the general public that they shouldn't care. But, and this has always been the case, historians don't have the luxury of autonomy (in fact, luxuries of all kinds seem to elude us). We can, at times, guide conversations, but we are also guided by the spirit of the times we inhabit.

This book, in addition to being prompted by an intriguing topic, is a response to cultural demands. Our questions about a possible wife of Jesus serve as a kind of cultural mirror. As we introduce new portraits of Jesus in popular novels, films, and so on, we also introduce a great deal of ourselves to these portraits.

In Bill Watterson's insightful (almost prophetic) comic strip "Calvin and Hobbes," he describes the troubling truth of writing history.[4] Calvin, a six-year-old boy with an overactive imagination and a self-awareness beyond his years, discusses historical revisionism with his friend Hobbes. Calvin observes, "History is the fiction that we invent to persuade ourselves that events are knowable and that life has order and direction." He continues to explain a key concept in postmodern historiography, this being the problem of "reinterpretation" when cultural values change. "We need new versions of history to allow for our current prejudices," argues Calvin. The punchline of the comic reveals that our favorite six-year-old is writing a revisionist autobiography.

Calvin is undoubtedly correct that "events are always reinterpreted when values change." But, as the punch line hints, historians must bring integrity to these cultural conversations, or risk absurdity. If our integrity cannot be measured by the foundations of past reality, it must be measured by our moral obligation to the present. To this end, I am reminded of the words of Yosef Hayim Yerushalmi:

> The burden of building a bridge to his people remains with the historian. I do not know for certain that this will be possible. I am convinced only that first the historian must truly desire it and then try to act accordingly . . . What historians choose to study and write about is obviously part of the problem. The notion that everything in the past is worth knowing "for its own sake" is a mythology of modern historians, as is the lingering suspicion that conscious responsibility toward the living concerns of the group must result in history that is less scholarly or "scientific." . . . Who, then, can be expected to step into the breach, if not the historian?[5]

The popularity of the topic of the wife of Jesus in our collective imagination demands a response from historians. Moreover, this topic deserves a response that builds a bridge between our collective imagination and historical memory. Yerushalmi knows what all historians ought to know: that we define ourselves by the histories we highlight. I think that there is no better time than now to have a clearer portrait of Jesus' sexuality.

This book is not another attempt to discover or invent an ancient personality who we can marry to Jesus. It is not a biography; *how could it be?*

I will put forward what I believe are the best arguments for and against a married Jesus. So, in this regard, I'm writing just another historical Jesus book. But no historical Jesus book is just about an ancient "him" – or, in this case, an ancient "her and him." At the same time, I am not immune to the intriguing possibility of a particular, historical wife of Jesus.

While this book is indeed about the possibility of a wife of Jesus, it is just as much about us: the Christianized West. Being a member of the Christianized West myself – and fascinated by the question of Jesus' sexuality – I acknowledge at the start that this topic is as much about "me and us" as it is about "her and him."

CHALLENGES

The various quests for the historical Jesus have always provided mirrors through which to view our own reflections. We've learned a great deal about the Jesus of history in these pursuits, but we've also learned a great deal about ourselves. We attempt to deconstruct and reconstruct our cultural icons because we want to know *how we got here* and *why*. Is it any wonder that we sexually preoccupied Westerners feel the need to rethink the sexuality of Jesus?

It is the *quest* for the wife of Jesus that intrigues – for the journey it will provide, not for the destination it might promise. So, as well as addressing the question 'was Jesus married?', this book will also attempt to answer the question: *what does it say about us that we're so fascinated and repulsed by this possibility?*

In the first century, many of Jesus' contemporaries were scandalized by the ascetic way of life. Indeed, the choice to avoid bread and wine made some people openly hostile to John the Baptist. John chose a life of asceticism and his contemporaries thought he had a demon. We tend to use more modern insults when we demonize each other, but those first-century debates over carnality versus asceticism have a great deal in common with our debates over tradition versus progress. Both then and now, Jesus is indicted and venerated by the company he keeps.

1

ACCORDING TO THE FLESH

"The Word became flesh and lived among us."
– THE GOSPEL OF JOHN

One reason why the topic of this book is controversial is because it implies that Jesus had a sexual identity. I think that many people view Jesus as a prototype for celibate priests. Many assume that Jesus chose celibacy for the same reason that priests take vows of celibacy. Sex is so commonly associated with naughtiness that it is difficult to think of it in terms of godliness. But, in our heart of hearts, we know that sex isn't sinful. So why is it so difficult to imagine a fully human Jesus who was married?

Could it be because we're projecting our own sexual hang-ups onto Jesus? Could it be that when we imagine Jesus with a sexual identity, we can't help but imagine a Jesus with the same sorts of hang-ups? Imagining a married Jesus feels a bit like we're defrocking Jesus – as if we're accusing him of failing to keep his vows.

But what if we think of Jesus not as a prototype for priests, but as an archetype for humanity? Indeed, at least for us Westerners, Jesus is an archetype. In this case, to say that Jesus is an "archetype" means that we use our ideas about him to create images of nobility, purity, and redemption. Put another way, our ideas about Jesus create a standard by which we measure our own nobility, purity, and redemption. Like it or not, this is the place that Jesus occupies in the Christianized West.

This is where things get tricky: if Jesus isn't sexual, how can we imagine our own sexual identities in noble, pure, and redemptive terms? If Jesus, the standard of nobility, is devoid of sexuality, how can we avoid feeling naughty? Could it be that we've created a non-sexual Jesus because of our own insecurities? Conversely, could it be that our continued insecurities have reinforced our image of a non-sexual Jesus?

WE'RE COMPLICATED

We Westerners are preoccupied with sex. Language can be a very important window into a culture. When something is interesting, we say it's "sexy." "Sex sells" is one of the mantras of democratic capitalism. One of our favorite storylines is "boy gets girl." Indeed, some of our most celebrated heroes are sexual conquerors of some sort: Rocky Balboa, James Bond, Robin Hood, Captain Kirk, Romeo, Superman, almost any film with John Wayne – the list could go on and on.

A dialogue from the HBO comedy series *Bored to Death* illustrates this idea of Western heroism. In the following scene a boyish, thirtysomething, would-be gumshoe is talking with a younger woman at a party:

> Her: "But are you a boy or a man?"
> Him: "A man ... [hesitates] what's the difference?"
> Her: "With a man, it's like he's taking you and you like it. With a boy it's like he's stealing something from you and you don't like it."

There are several levels of absurdity in this exchange, but I'll only point to one. Here we see that the woman *is the conquest*. It's not that she is a partner in the hero's journey; she is the boon, the object that the boy can claim to make him a hero.

Of course, we can think of exceptions. For example, in the Coen brother's film *The Big Lebowski*, the hero is all but disinterested in becoming a sexual conqueror. Consider this portrait from the script:

> "And I'm talkin' about The Dude here . . . even if he's a lazy man, and The Dude was certainly that – quite possibly the laziest man in Los Angeles County, which would place him high in the running for the laziest worldwide . . ."[1]

But this is the exception that proves the rule; "The Dude" is entertaining because of his utter lack of drive. More often than not, we want our heroes to be conquerors, and this is commonly shown as sexual conquest.

The flip side of this coin is that we Westerners are terrified of sex. Sexuality is on display in almost every kind of media and, ironically, it is a source of shame for us. It is often difficult for us to talk about sex intergenerationally. Sometimes we even have trouble talking about sex with our sexual partners. We have very few sacred rites of passage to nurture our children to maturity. We fear the idea of our children maturing because we fear how they might explore their sexual identities.

Worse, we tend to forbid or problematize language that speaks to sex directly. This is another way that language provides a window into our culture. For good or ill, the heroes of our favorite narratives communicate our ideals and aspirations for us. This is not to sermonize against art; it is just an observation of our cultural complexity. Because we refuse to talk about sex directly, we give the image of James Bond more power by default.[2]

In my view, the loss of tradition that infuses sexuality with sacred significance is a problem. The heroes of popular culture have reinforced the myth of conquest that dehumanizes women. At the same time, the traditionally religious voices have lost almost all credibility in public discourse. For example, the Catholic Church has lost considerable ground on topics related to sexual norms (especially in recent years). But many still long for a religious institution with a long view. Many, including me, like the idea of an institution that isn't blown over by every passing inclination of popular culture. I like the idea of sacred rites of passage that help us pass down sacraments from generation to generation. I don't want my children to fear sex or pretend to be non-sexual, nor do I want them to buy into the myth of sexual conquest.

The Church has traditionally championed a Jesus who isn't conquest-oriented. The history of Christianity has been a story of conquest in many ways; but the image of the defeated Jesus, hung on a Roman cross as a willing and altruistic sacrifice is a different type of hero. For this subversive image I am grateful to Catholicism and I am reluctant to let go of the image. But the traditionally non-sexual, celibate portrait of Jesus works hand-in-glove with this image. In Western iconography, Jesus is not a conquistador. Images of him that suggest otherwise are intriguing because they are novel. But, at the end of the day, would a married Jesus really destroy this image? Must sexuality always be about our imperfections?

Christianity has both contributed to and critiqued our popular views of sexuality in the West. This is important to recognize because the discussion of a married Jesus will have consequences. Psychologist and theological theorist Hal Childs writes that we quest for Jesus' personality to see our collective, psychological "reflection at the bottom of the well."[3] Saying anything "new" about Jesus reveals something about us. According to Childs, Jesus reflects the face of God to us; at the same time, Jesus reflects our own humanity back to us. In art, religion, indeed Western culture at large, Jesus is the portrait of complete and authentic humanity. And yet he represents a humanity that is devoid of sexuality. Something is amiss.

Christ on the Cross (1631), Rembrandt van Rijn. This oil on canvas painting of Christ borrows the classic and iconic image of cruciformity but conveys Jesus in anguish. This emotion and the dramatic use of light seeks to draw the viewer into the scene through empathy. These are common features of the (high) Baroque period. The Roman Catholic Church of this period was invested in communicating basic religious themes through direct, emotionally expressive, and engaging paintings like this.

Perhaps, when it comes to sexuality, Jesus is a hero that reflects our innocence, and we are reluctant to see him as fully human. A married Jesus will have consequences on several levels because of how important he has become in defining our sexual norms and values. In my opinion, we really don't need a James Bond type of Jesus. Perhaps we need – as the Church has always known – a fully human Jesus. At the same time, we should be wary of inventing a sexuality for Jesus simply because we want to assuage our own insecurities.

THE EMERGENCE OF ASCETIC RELIGION

Jesus was a first-century, Jewish Galilean. It is probable that he did not come from a well-educated or cosmopolitan family.[4] Many of his views about sex and family would have been informed by deeply rooted traditions and by rural rabbis. While this provides us with a starting point, it does not tell us everything we need to know about Jesus. A large part of being Jewish involves negotiating with non-Jewish religions and cultures. This has been true throughout the history of Judaism and was certainly true during the time of Jesus.

Long before Jesus walked the Earth, and the Apostle Paul wrote his letters, Alexander the Great ruled from Egypt to Pakistan. Greek language, philosophy, sports, politics, and culture more generally seeped through the cracks of thousands of clans. Greek culture in Alexander's empire was much like capitalism is today in our "global" economy. There are a few standard ways of thinking, and a thousand different adaptations.

One of the more common ideas during the period of Greek domination was that gods could be *and often were* sexual beings. This was a notion that the Greeks probably borrowed from the Egyptians. Fertility is fundamental for life, and thus sexuality is fundamental for human life. We see this idea reflected in Egyptian mythology, Greek mythology, and Roman mythology. The sexuality of gods wasn't just a quirky or obscure notion. This idea was commonplace in the history of Western culture from before 3000 B.C.E. and only waned during the rise of Christianity and Islam. Unlike the God of the Hebrew Bible,[5] many other gods of the Mediterranean world were sexual beings.

Judaism has always had to negotiate with neighboring religious expressions and this has included negotiating with various expressions of sexuality. This was no less true in the time of Jesus and Paul. But what was relatively new during this period of Western civilization was widespread religious "asceticism."

ASCETICISM

As mentioned previously, asceticism is the belief that a new and better self can emerge when a person withdraws from normal life (variously defined). Ascetic expression also included the practice of physical deprivation. Ascetics in Greek culture often deprived themselves of food, comfort, family, and sex, believing that they could achieve a more advanced spirituality by doing so.

Many ascetics believed that the physical world was evil and that the human spirit was hindered by physical appetites. While this is a common religious expression in Jainism and Buddhism, Greek asceticism developed from athletic training and philosophy. Within this general life ethic, abstinence from sex was thought to open the possibility for a better spiritual existence. So the philosophical inclination to view sex as evil was already thriving in the sixth century B.C.E., but it took a few more centuries for it to become a widespread *religious* expression.[6]

Because Judaism was always negotiating with neighboring religions and cultures, Jewish life took on different forms in different times and places. In short, there were many ways to live a Jewish life during Jesus' time. In addition to the many fertility rituals that were practiced throughout the Mediterranean, there were other groups that attempted to abstain from sex altogether.

Some Jews were quite interested in Greek philosophy and some were less interested. And in the midst of this plurality, most Jews attempted to observe the very first commandment given by God to humanity in the Hebrew Bible: "Be fruitful and multiply." A traditionally Jewish view would have acknowledged the intrinsic goodness of the physical world. Sex would have been seen as a requirement from this perspective. Many Jewish teachers would have also seen sex as a source of pleasure as well. Consider the Jewish saying found in the book of Proverbs:

> Let your fountain be blessed,
> and rejoice in the wife of your youth,
> a lovely deer; a graceful doe.
> May her breasts satisfy you at all times;
> may you be intoxicated always by her love.[7]

The Jewish sage who wrote this encourages sexual expression for the sake of conjugal pleasure. He cautions against adultery, but (much like the Song of Songs) promotes a wider view of sexuality, complete with foreplay. For the author of this proverb, at least, sexual pleasure was not simply a by-product of procreation. Moreover, and most importantly, sexual pleasure was not seen as a sin that hindered one's religious life.

Yet we know that some Jews during the time of Jesus and Paul became advocates of a more ascetic life, forsaking physical pleasure – and marriage along with it. Perhaps, as I've already suggested, John the Baptist is an example of this. While it would be misleading to paint Jewish life in the extremes of hedonism or asceticism, what can be said with a fairly high degree of confidence is that Judaism adopted or adapted several forms of Greek (and Persian) dualism in the centuries leading up to the birth of Christianity. Specifically, the belief that humanity was dual in nature – existing as both body and soul – was highly influential.

Judaism in that time and place included many Roman and Greek-influenced ways of life. I emphasize this because the Greeks and Romans had a wide range of ideas about sexuality, and some of these influenced the development of Christianity. Many early Christians incorporated ascetic expressions into their religion. A Roman physician and philosopher named Galen observed this of Christians: "They include not only men but also women who refrain from cohabitating all through their lives; and they also number individuals who, in self-discipline and self-control in matters of food and drink, and in their keen pursuit of justice, have attained a pitch not inferior to that of the genuine philosophers."[8] While Galen offers us a second-century perspective, it is quite likely that some of the earliest non-Jewish followers of Jesus were motivated by asceticism. Letters to the Christians in Corinth and to Timothy (among others) suggest that many Christians thought that sexuality was physical as opposed to spiritual.

There were also rumors that some Christians participated in orgies wherein husbands and wives would swing from one partner to the next. These rumors were widespread enough to warrant multiple Christian writers to refute them. Indeed, if Paul's writings on the topic of Christian liberty were to be taken to an extreme, one can easily imagine this sort of sexually ecstatic worship in some Christian communities.

But Paul, the person most responsible for bringing Christianity to the non-Jewish world, writes in response to what he sees as extreme forms of sexuality among his contemporaries. He argues that extremes are problematic. Paul is critical of Christians who showed too little restraint, and was equally critical of those who tried to force celibacy onto others. That said, although deeply committed to Judaism, Paul seems to have been influenced by Greek culture in a number of ways. For example, he seems to have chosen a temporary life of celibacy during his missionary career. Paul does not think that marriage is evil, and seems open to the idea of getting married himself at some point.[9] But it is important to recognize that the idea of celibacy would have seemed antithetical to Jewish life prior to Greek influence. It seems that many Jewish religious leaders during Jesus' time struggled between Greek ideals and the constraints and liberties of traditional Jewish instruction (what we might loosely call "Torah"). My point here is a simple one: the more that Christianity became non-Jewish (more often than not, anti-Jewish), the less it was oriented toward traditional Jewish instruction about sexuality.

EXAMPLES OF CHRISTIAN ASCETICISM

The topic of Christian asceticism will be revisited often throughout this book. I will offer only a few examples here to illustrate the general development of the tradition. Consider an early Christian story found in a book called *The Shepherd of Hermas*. This text was very influential in many Christian circles in the second and third centuries. In fact, it was included alongside the Gospels and the letters of Paul in some cases. In *Hermas*, a religious pilgrim finds himself in the care of twelve virgins while he waits for his spiritual guide called "the shepherd." Here is an excerpt from chapter eleven:

> The virgins said to me, "The Shepherd does not come here today." "What, then," said I, "am I to do?" They replied, "Wait for him until he comes; and if he comes he will converse with you, and if he does not come you will remain here with us until he does come." I said to them, "I will wait for him until it is late; and if he does not arrive, I will go away into the house, and come back early in the morning." And they answered and said to me, "You were entrusted to us; you cannot go away from us." "Where, then," I said, "am I to remain?" "You will sleep with us," they replied, "as a brother, and not as a husband: for you are our brother, and for the time to come we intend to abide with you, for we love you exceedingly!"

But I was ashamed to remain with them. And she who seemed to be the first among them began to kiss me. And the others seeing her kissing me, began also to kiss me, and to lead me round the tower, and to play with me. And I, too, became like a young man, and began to play with them: for some of them formed a chorus, and others danced, and others sang; and I, keeping silence, walked with them around the tower, and was merry with them. And when it grew late I wished to go into the house; and they would not let me, but detained me. So I remained with them during the night, and slept beside the tower.

Now the virgins spread their linen tunics on the ground, and made me lie down in the midst of them; and they did nothing at all but pray; and I without ceasing prayed with them, and not less than they. And the virgins rejoiced because I thus prayed. And I remained there with the virgins until the next day at the second hour.

The spiritual shepherd returns to find that the pilgrim has remained chaste. He has kissed, danced, and slept alongside a dozen naked virgins. But he has climaxed in prayer rather than coitus. This story has several parallels with Greek erotic literature but takes on an especially ascetic tone. If you're familiar with the film *The Big Lebowski*, you'll find a few parallels there too.[10]

The Shepherd of Hermas was eventually excluded from the New Testament, but the ideals expressed in this story became integral for non-Jewish Christianity. To abstain from sex was holy. Celibacy in the face of temptation was heroic. Sin and sex became almost synonymous after Christianity and Judaism parted ways.

Saint Jerome is often pointed to as the crusader against sex and women in general. He argued that marriage was the result of sin and that sex was a necessary evil. His views on marriage are more nuanced than is normally recognized, but his basic belief was that "virginity is natural while wedlock only follows guilt."[11] But pointing to a few especially misogynistic quotes from Jerome can obscure how prevalent this logic was in mainstream Christianity.

Augustine of Hippo, perhaps the most influential theologian in the history of Christianity, rejected the idea that the human body, and the physical world in general, was evil: "For the soul and the body, and all the natural endowments which are implanted in the soul and the body, even in the persons of sinful men, are still gifts of God."[12] Augustine, unlike many ascetic Christians, supported the idea of marriage. But Augustine never fully embraced the virtue of sexual pleasure in the way that the author of Proverbs 5 suggests. Augustine encouraged married couples to abstain from sex unless it was for the purpose of procreation. He wrote: 'The union, then, of male and female for the purpose of procreation is the natural good of marriage. But he makes a bad use of this good who uses it bestially, so that his intention is on the gratification of lust, instead of the desire of offspring.'[13]

Notice here Augustine's either/or mentality. *Either* sex is motivated by the desire for children *or* it is beastly. Augustine is generally remembered as the Christian champion against asceticism. But here we see a carryover. He is clearly suspicious of sexual pleasure when pursued for its own sake. This view, represented with prominence by Augustine, became the standard for Christianity.

Almost a millennium later, theologian Thomas Aquinas reflected on Augustine's view of sexuality. Aquinas wrote: "The exceeding pleasure attaching to a venereal act, directed according to reason, is not opposed to the mean of virtue."[14] Here, Aquinas defends sexual pleasure. It is not, he argues, to be reduced to lust when it is experienced "according to reason." For Aquinas, such pleasure was reasonable when it was done for the purpose of procreation. Again, we see that even the least ascetic Christian theologians were unable to commend sexual pleasure without reservation.

The history of Christianity has included a long and robust debate about sexuality. There have been prominent voices on either side of this debate. But the reason that the debate was necessary in the first place is because the Church adopted and adapted Greek asceticism. The belief that the physical world was only a shade of a higher reality – and that therefore physical pleasure is to be shunned – is not a teaching that came from Jesus.

PHANTOM JESUS

After centuries of debate, the voices that affirmed the essential goodness of the creation and creatures won. Christians such as Marcion (c. 85–c. 160), who argued that the God of the "Old Testament" was a demiurge (a lesser god) who created an evil world, lost the debate. Christians like Augustine, who affirmed the claim of Genesis that all creation was created with inherent goodness, won the debate. In this case, the "winners" wrote the doctrines that would provide a foundation for Christianity.

But before the losers were obscured by historians, these "heretics" were quite successful at reinventing a non-physical Jesus. Their logic can be summed up like this: because the physical world is evil, Jesus could not have been physical. Their Jesus never left footprints when he walked. He was an entirely spiritual being who wore a mask of physicality. Some even argued that Jesus never had a bowel movement because he had super-special innards! A Christian named Valentinus (c. 100–c. 160) is purported to have said: 'Jesus digested divinity; he ate and drank in a special way, without excreting his solids. He had such a great capacity for continence that the nourishment within him was not corrupted, for he did not experience corruption.'[15]

While it is difficult to reconstruct the thinking of Valentinus with any confidence, this saying at least illustrates a popular portrait of

Jesus in the second century. For many Christians, Jesus could only be pure if he was without physicality.

Around one hundred years after Jesus' crucifixion, Christians began debates about his celibacy. Tatian was a second-century theologian who (following the lead of Justin Martyr) argued that Jesus never married. While Tatian was labeled a heretic for many of his views, his idea about Jesus' celibacy became entrenched in popular Christianity. It is worth noting that Tatian also taught that Satan invented sex and that Adam (not God) instituted the union of Adam and Eve. In the latter half of the second century, Clement of Alexandria offered a response to this view:

> There are those who say openly that marriage is fornication.
> They lay it down as a dogma that it was instituted by the devil.
> They are arrogant and claim to be emulating the Lord [Christ]
> who did not marry and had no earthly possessions. They do
> not know the reason why the Lord did not marry. In the first
> place, he had his own bride, the Church. Secondly, he was not
> a common man to need a physical partner. Further, he did not
> have an obligation to produce children; he was born God's
> only son and survives eternally.[16]

Here, Clement reacts to the view that marriage is a concession to our carnal natures. He has his own reasons to believe that Jesus was celibate. Clement's rationale will be revisited elsewhere in this book. For now, notice that *both* Clement and these supposed heretics assume that Jesus did not marry. Clement's assumption of Jesus' celibacy suggests that – by the second century – many Christians assumed that Jesus never married; it was the question "why not?" that fueled debate. If so, do these second-century debates tell us something of Jesus' first-century reputation?[17]

While Christian doctrine eventually celebrated the full humanity of Jesus, the invention of Jesus' celibacy on ascetic grounds would have a long legacy within Christianity. This belief seems to stem from the anti-physical and anti-sexual ideologies made popular in the second century. These early ascetic Christians could not imagine a wife of Jesus because they were convinced that Jesus shunned physical pleasure and comfort. In some cases, this ascetic Jesus wasn't even flesh and blood, but entirely spirit. But the portraits of Jesus from our earliest documents suggest that his physicality was affirmed even by those who were earnestly convinced that Jesus was divine.

Paul repeats the early Christian belief that Jesus was "born according to the flesh." Our earliest documents suggest that Jesus was not an ascetic, but was known for drinking and feasting. The ascetic foundations for the belief in Jesus' celibacy do not square with the earliest portraits of Jesus.

CHALLENGES

The apostolic church and professional historians have always claimed interest in Jesus' "full humanity." But any theology or history that portrays a Jesus devoid of sexual identity falls short of the task. Jesus may well have chosen a life of celibacy, but to build this claim upon the assumption that sex is sinful is faulty. Moreover, the hope that a celibate life might diminish or "solve" one's sexual nature is a pious deception.

The certainty of Jesus' celibacy by second-century Christians was misguided. Whatever conclusion is forwarded concerning Jesus' marital status, we must acknowledge that the traditional assumptions for Jesus' celibacy are unsustainable. It may be impossible to pursue the topic of this book objectively, but I believe that it is possible to do so honestly. Honesty compels me to observe that (1) second-century Christian assumptions about sexuality were generally damaging to their portraits of Jesus and (2) the impact that these assumptions had on the Christianized West were wildly successful, to ill effect.

That said, we should be aware of our own agendas. Are we to lean toward Jesus' celibacy because tradition is on our side? Do we quest for a wife of Jesus because we're repulsed by Christian asceticism? Are we preconditioned to "discover" Jesus' wife because we need an archetype that can provide symbolic value for our shifting views of sexuality? Is it possible that we aim to invent a married Jesus because our favorite heroes are sexual conquistadors?

It might not be possible to remove these kinds of biases. All historical quests are inevitably laden with ideological baggage. But we should, at least, be aware of the questions we bring with us on this quest.

FURTHER READING

Peter Brown, *The Body and Society: Men, Women, and Sexual Renunciation in Early Christianity* (New York: Columbia University Press, 1988).

Elizabeth Clark (ed.), *St. Augustine on Marriage and Sexuality: Selections from the Fathers of the Church* (Washington D.C.: Catholic University of America Press, 1996).

James D. G. Dunn, *Christian Liberty: A New Testament Perspective: The Didsbury Lectures* (Carlisle: Paternoster Press, 1993).

Alexander R. Pruss, *One Body: An Essay in Christian Sexual Ethics; ND Studies in Ethics and Culture* (Notre Dame, IN: University of Notre Dame Press, 2012).

Vincent L. Wimbush and Richard Valantasis (eds), *Asceticism* (Oxford: Oxford University Press, 1998).

2

Substance and Shadow

*"In human intercourse the tragedy begins, not when
there is misunderstanding about words, but
when silence is not understood."*

– HENRY DAVID THOREAU

The texts of the New Testament have traditionally been seen as the most authoritative witnesses to the life of Jesus. Both professional historians and mainstream theologians have pointed to Matthew, Mark, Luke, and John as preserving the earliest and best data. Many historians now argue that the *Gospel of Thomas* (not in the New Testament) is among the earliest. Probably earlier than all of these Gospels are the letters of Paul. It should be said at the start that none of these texts tell us that Jesus was married. Paul's letters, Matthew, Mark, Luke, John, Thomas – none of these refer to a literal wife of Jesus.

But, and this point is equally important, the Gospels and the rest of these texts *do not tell us that Jesus was single*. As I discussed in chapter 1, our default is to assume that Jesus was celibate. The burden of proof is on those who would suggest otherwise. I would challenge this assumption. If our earliest and best sources do not speak concerning Jesus' marital status, assumptions of his celibacy are unwarranted. After arguments from both sides are heard, we may well conclude that Jesus was celibate, but both sides should share the burden of proof equally.

I say "*should* share the burden of proof." *Should,* of course, does not make something so. The fact of the matter is that the iconic Jesus of the Christianized West has been celibate for almost two millennia. Surely the burden of proof will be on those who would challenge this portrait. And so it is left to the historian to explain the silence of our sources concerning Jesus' marital status: *If Jesus had a wife, why don't we know her name? Why don't we hear a single word from her? Why doesn't Jesus refer to her in his teachings?*

If one begins with the default position of a celibate Jesus (and most people begin precisely here), these are questions that demand answers.

THE PROBLEMS OF SILENCE

The voices of women are most often unheard within the histories of men. There are exceptions, but the rule is primary. We don't see many statues commemorating great women; we don't celebrate many holidays in honor of women; we are much less inclined to remember the women who have shaped our cultural landscapes. This reality is undoubtedly true in the development of the Western world where "the most valued recollections remain only those that are inherently male."[1]

So it should come as no great surprise that the mothers, sisters, daughters, and wives of ancient times are most often obscured. Indeed, I often challenge my students to think of an ancient heroine who is not primarily known as the wife, sister, daughter, or mother of a more famous male. There are a handful of exceptions, but not many.

The annals of history may have obscured the names and voices of important figures, but sometimes these nameless people still speak to us.

Take, for example, a poem written by Fu Xüan (c. 217–78 C.E.) titled "Woman."[2] The poem introduces the topic as a lament: "How sad it is to be a woman! Nothing on earth is held so cheap." From this perspective, the lament relates to the entire family and is directly related to financial concerns: "No one is glad when a girl is born: by her the family gets no store." The perspective of the poem purports to be feminine: "Boys stand leaning at the door; Like gods fallen out of Heaven." In the face of her male luminaries, the woman must remain silent, and subservient, "Her teeth are pressed on her red lips." Finally, the woman receives derivative self-worth from her husband, but this proves to be an illusion and fleeting: "A hundred evils are heaped upon her . . . Her lord will find new pleasures." The final lament is perhaps the most heartbreaking, as the poem describes the eventual distance between herself and her husband: "They that were once like substance and shadow are now as far as Hu from Ch'in."[3] This poem offers a general expression of womanhood during the Han and Three Kingdoms periods in China (contemporary with the rise of Christianity). The poet demonstrates the problem of silence in at least two ways. The most obvious problem is on the surface of the text. The woman in this portrait humbly keeps her lips pressed. She is observant, subservient, only a shadow. Her worth is derived from her lord and is ultimately fleeting. Even at the best of times, her relationship with him is that of "substance and shadow."

The second problem illustrated here is that of authorship. For all of the empathy that Fu Xüan engenders, this poem was composed by a man. The woman's perspective is enclosed within a man's voice. As subversive as this poem might sound, the act of speaking on behalf of a silent woman might be another way to preserve her silence.[4]

One could say that this poem is a portrait of a faceless and nameless woman. It is a problem that weighs heavily on me because one could say the same of the cover art and title of this book. On the one hand, this poem reflects the man who wrote it; on the other, the poem provides an irresistible historical portrait. Fu Xüan's nameless woman is simply too compelling to dismiss.

More often than not, the ancients obscure the names and voices that we're eager to discover. But the problem is also with us moderns. Take, for example, a woman who lived about one hundred years before Jesus. Her name was Shelamzion and she ruled as the Queen of Israel for over ten years. Shelamzion held together a fractured people, charged into battle, led her armies to victory, and was wildly popular among her people for generations after her death. She inherited from her husband a kingdom on the brink of anarchy – and improved her people's fortunes. After her reign, Israel deteriorated quickly. The mismanagement of her sons led to internal conflicts and left Israel's borders weak. After the departure of Shelamzion, Israel would not regain political autonomy until 1948.

Shelamzion "Salome" Alexandra: *the last queen of Israel.* Her remarkable story is the stuff of legend; yet she is almost entirely unknown to most modern people.[5] This is not for a lack of references to her; she is mentioned in ancient histories, rabbinic literature, and in the Dead Sea Scrolls. The reason that her name is largely unknown to us is not the fault of ancient historians. Sometimes, we modern and "enlightened" folk are to blame for the silence of women in history. And if a woman as extraordinary as Shelamzion can become nameless and voiceless, what chance do first-century peasants have? The silence of women in history is an ancient and modern problem.

In the case of a possible wife of Jesus, our earliest sources do not address Jesus' marital status. But we should *not* assume that silence is evidence of Jesus' celibacy. Silenced women, obscured women – these are the lamentable rules of history. On the other hand, we should not simply assume that the silence concerning Jesus' marital status indicates that he was married. The early Christians were not silent on the subject of marriage and family. Jesus himself was not silent about this topic, and much of what he said suggests a negative view of the institution. Our quest for the wife of Jesus might begin with silence, but it must account for the cacophony of voices that border this void.

NAMELESS WIVES AND SISTERS

Allow me to address a question that a friend asked me recently: "How is it possible that Jesus could have had a wife, but she is never mentioned in the Gospels?" Framed in another way, we could ask: *Is it conceivable that Christianity, a movement that honored and commemorated the names of several women in leadership, could have entirely obscured the wife of Jesus?*

Not only is this possible, it is likely that several important women were eclipsed by the commemoration of the early Jesus movement. I will give two examples: (1) Jesus' sisters and (2) Peter's wife.

Every indication from the New Testament is that Jesus was the firstborn among several siblings.[6] Jesus' brothers, most notably James, became leaders in early Christianity. But what of his sisters? Aside from a brief mention of them in the Gospel of Mark, we might never have known that Jesus had sisters. Mark tells a story set early in Jesus' public career. Jesus' neighbors are amazed and perhaps a bit skeptical of his budding career as a preacher and faith healer. Jesus is acting like a religious and prophetic authority, and yet he comes from a family of craftsmen. They ask: is not this the carpenter, the son of Mary, and brother of James and Joses and Judas and Simon? Are not his sisters here with us?[7]

His neighbors mention Mary (his mother), James, Joses, Judas, and Simon by name, but Jesus' sisters remain nameless.[8] They are an afterthought. This simply confirms what the historian expects. Either these names weren't important enough to remember, or the author didn't imagine that the reader would care.

Some scholars have suggested that this episode from Mark is where we might expect to hear of Jesus' wife, if he had one. But such expectations are misplaced. Jesus' neighbors point to Jesus' blood relatives to emphasize that they know where he comes from. He and his family are artisans, not scholars, not religious leaders. More to the point, we know that some of Jesus' brothers were married (more on this below) – and Mark neglects to mention any wives in this passage. The sisters are nameless and the wives are omitted altogether. It could be that there were simply no wives to mention. Clearly, this passage cannot be used as evidence that Jesus or his brothers were married during his public career. But it most certainly does not provide proof that they were celibate.

An even more telling omission is the example of Peter's wife. Peter, also called "Cephas," is the most celebrated of Jesus' disciples. He has the most speaking roles in the Gospels and was an important leader in early Jewish Christianity. From a Catholic perspective, Peter is listed as the first pope. It is worth pointing out that we do not hear from most of the disciples of Jesus; the Gospels list various disciples who are never given speaking roles. Given this relative silence by the disciples, Peter's role is magnified by the Gospels. We are told that he was in the fishing business, but we know very little else about Peter's life before he joined Jesus' movement.

One thing we do know, however, is that Peter was married. We know this despite the fact that his wife is never mentioned in the Gospels. The Gospels of Matthew, Mark, and Luke mention Peter's ill mother-in-law.[9] So while there is no mention of Peter's wife directly, we can infer that he was married from the fact that he had a mother-in-law. Paul's first letter to the Corinthians confirms Peter's marital status

Healing of Peter's Mother-in-Law (*c.* 1660), Rembrandt van Rijn. Rembrandt often chose specific biblical episodes to create visual studies. In this case, we see the scene described in Matthew: "When Jesus entered Peter's house, he saw his mother-in-law lying in bed with a fever ... This was to fulfill what had been spoken through the prophet Isaiah, 'He took our infirmities and bore our diseases.'" (Matt 8:14, 17)

with a passing comment about Peter's marriage. Paul argues that he himself has the right to get married if he so chooses, just like Peter. He asks rhetorically: "Do we [Paul is speaking of himself] not have a right to be accompanied by a believing wife, even as the rest of the apostles and the brothers of the Lord and Cephas?"[10]

Paul knows of Peter's marital status, but does not refer to Peter's wife directly. She remains a shadow in the annals of history. She had a husband, a mother, she becomes a precedent for Paul – but she has been eclipsed. It is not Peter's wife that we hear about, but Peter's marital status. I assume no ill will on the part of Paul; his letters are focused efforts on particular topics and this is just a passing comment. My point is simply that if Paul were not so preoccupied with defending himself and his claim to apostleship, he might not have mentioned Peter's marital status. That we know of her existence at all is a remarkable exception to the rule.

We also learn from Paul that the disciples (called "apostles") of Jesus were married. It seems that even the most important leaders of this religious movement were married (or at least were married at some point in their lives). Paul acknowledges that he is the odd exception in choosing (temporarily?) celibacy, but he reserves the right to be married just like the others. It is worth noting, however, that second-century theologian Clement argues that Paul was married.[11]

Paul also assumes that Jesus' brothers were married. To put it as plainly as possible: it is highly likely that all of the first apostles were married, that Jesus' brothers were married, and yet we never meet their wives in the pages of the New Testament. If Jesus had a wife at some point, it would not be surprising that we never hear from her or about her. For a Jewish religious leader in antiquity to be married and for his wife to be completely ignored is lamentable, but shouldn't surprise us in the least.

THE WISDOM OF SALOME

Without question, many early members of Jesus' following were eclipsed by characters such as Peter and John. But it would be misleading to paint an entirely negative picture of the Jesus traditions. Some stories about the life of Jesus break from the typical patterns of misogyny in a number of ways.

A great deal has been written about Mary, the Mother of Jesus, and Mary Magdalene (both are key characters in the narratives), but lesser known among the followers of Jesus is a woman named Salome. She is not to be confused with the many other Salomes from this period. The follower of Jesus by this name is mentioned twice in the Gospel of Mark and once in the *Gospel of Thomas*. In *Thomas*, Salome declares herself a "disciple" of Jesus. This designation is usually reserved for the men associated with apostleship.

In the Gospel of Mark – the first narrative of Jesus' life – Salome is among the traveling companions of Jesus. She has followed him to Jerusalem and eventually witnesses his execution. She is also among the women who attempt to tend to Jesus' corpse only to find the tomb empty. Salome is thus a witness to two of the most celebrated events in the life of Jesus: his death and resurrection. Yet her character never appears again in the New Testament.

The silence of Salome, however, is broken in a text called the *Proto-Gospel of James*. At least, a character named Salome enters this narrative and witnesses another great moment in the life of Jesus: his birth. Perhaps the author reasoned that if Salome had seen the death and empty tomb, she ought to have witnessed Jesus' birth as well.

The *Proto-Gospel of James* (also called the *Protoevangelium of James*) is a second-century historical fiction that centers on Mary, the mother of Jesus. One might think of it as a "prequel" to the canonical Gospels, as it purports to describe events that happened before and during the birth of Jesus. This story tells of Mary's birth and marriage at the age of twelve to Joseph. It assumes that Joseph had children by a previous marriage. The text seems to exhibit a high "Mariology" – in other words, Mary is venerated highly in this text, and a defense of her perpetual virginity is launched. The text seems to rely on Matthew, Mark, and Luke for information about Jesus' birth, but portrays the birth of Jesus in a cave.

As the story goes, Joseph and Mary were traveling when Mary begins to feel the pressure of childbirth. In this version of the story, Joseph finds a cave for Mary to "hide her shame." Mary gives birth to Jesus, but in such a way that miraculously leaves her hymen intact. A local midwife comes to examine Mary and is amazed. Then Salome enters the scene.

The midwife went out of the cave and Salome met her. And she said to her, "Salome, Salome, I can describe a new wonder to you. A virgin has given birth, contrary to her natural condition." Salome replied, "As the Lord my God lives, if I do not insert my finger and examine her condition, I will not believe that the virgin has given birth." The midwife went in and said to Mary, "Brace yourself, for there is no small controversy concerning you." Then Salome inserted her finger in order to examine her condition, and she cried out, "Woe to me for my sin and faithlessness! For I have tested (or tempted) the living God, and see, my hand is burning, falling away from me!"[12]

Salome then prays for mercy and an angel appears to her. The angel instructs her to pick up the baby Jesus. When she does, she worships him and her hand is healed. She also vows to keep secret this miracle until Jesus enters Jerusalem (presumably, in his adulthood). This last detail suggests that this fictional Salome is based on the character at the end of Mark's Gospel. Perhaps the silence of Salome, named prominently but with no real personality in Mark's Gospel, was too much to bear for early Christians. When silenced by historical memory, historical fiction filled in the gaps.

A person named Salome also becomes a central character in a text called the *Gospel of the Egyptians*. No manuscripts from this gospel survived, but it is quoted by Clement of Alexandria in the late second century. Based on what we can reconstruct of this gospel,

Salome and Jesus discuss childbirth: "When Salome asked, 'How long will death prevail?' the Lord [Jesus] replied, 'For as long as you women bear children.'"[13]

Jesus' response reflects a common idea about childbirth that Christianity adopted, probably reflecting a second-century mythology.[14] For now, I will simply note that in both of these early fictions, Salome is connected with the topics of childbirth and sin. In the *Gospel of the Egyptians* she is instructed on this matter (with misogynistic undertones) by Jesus. In the *Proto-Gospel of James,* Salome is instructed on the purity and virginity of Mary, implying that Jesus was not born in impurity or sin.[15] Salome's prominence but silence in Mark's Gospel probably piqued the curiosities of many early Christians, who were scandalized by the idea of a woman "disciple." Salome, then, became the spokesperson for the sinful cycle perpetuated by childbirth.[16]

Salome also has a minor speaking role in the *Gospel of Thomas.* Like many sayings in *Thomas,* the conversation is presented with very little context. We also run into the problem of gaps in the text. Here is the exchange:

> Jesus said, "Two will rest on a bed: the one will die, and the other will live." Salome said, "Who are you, man, that you . . . have come up on my bed and eaten from my table?" Jesus said to her, "I am he who exists from the undivided. I was given some of the things of my Father" . . . "I am your disciple" . . . "Therefore I say, if he is destroyed he will be filled with light, but if he is divided, he will be filled with darkness."[17]

While the references to two "on a bed" and Jesus resting on Salome's bed might indicate eroticism, it is more likely that the implied setting is a public feast. This is not to say that ancient

Mediterranean parties couldn't include both food and sex, but Jesus and Salome seem to be reclining during a meal in this episode. In either case, this portrait of Jesus shows him making himself at home in Salome's house.

While this saying probably does not reflect a historical event, it does provide us with some very intriguing historical information. It may even fill out a number of details about Salome and Jesus. This saying, while probably fictive, lends support to the probability that:

1. Jesus often attended parties.
2. Jesus often conversed with women as a rabbi would with a disciple.
3. A woman named Salome was among Jesus' companions.
4. Jesus accepted hospitality and support from women.

On this last point, we should remember that the Gospel of Luke puts forth the picture of Jesus traveling and preaching alongside his twelve apostles and many women. These included Mary Magdalene, Joanna, Susanna, "and many others, who provided for them out of their resources."[18] While not named in Luke, Salome's portrait in *Thomas* would fit Luke's profile. This is probably what Mark has in mind when Salome is named specifically and depicted as providing "for him when he was in Galilee."[19]

Salome is the rare exception: a woman who is mentioned by name and remembered independently of a male relative.[20] She is not explicitly named as the sister, or mother, or aunt, or wife of a more famous disciple. While later Christian authors attempted to categorize her as a female relative to one of the men in these stories, she is an independent disciple in the Gospel of Mark, *Gospel of Thomas, Proto-Gospel of James,* and *Gospel of the Egyptians.*[21]

Anne Lapidus Lerner observes something very similar in Eve's legacy: "Eve enters the biblical narrative as a dimly perceived shadow. She is subsumed in the *adam*, the first human . . . Eve's trajectory moves from obscurity, to real power, falling precipitously" in subsequent narratives.[22] One could say something very similar about the trajectory of characterization applied to Salome in Christianity. Salome enters in obscurity, rises to prominence in the imagination among early Christians, and then becomes a vehicle to explain how sin enters the world.

What is fictionalized about Salome is her role in misogynist propaganda. She becomes a foil to degrade the purity of childbirth and womanhood in general. Her silence made her a blank slate upon which general indictments of women could be written. Her historical portrait is that of an independent disciple, important in her own right. The historical fictions about her use her as a prop. This procedure will need to be remembered as we consider Mary Magdalene's legacy.

THE SOUND OF SILENCE

Israeli scholar Tal Ilan writes: "The techniques used to diminish and silence women are many and varied."[23] In this chapter I have only touched on a few of these techniques. What is equally important about Ilan's observation is that she recognizes that not every silence betrays a typical scenario. In other words, while historians have been typically myopic, not every historian is silent for the same reason. To extend this line of nuance, I will risk an obvious statement: sometimes silence is just silence.

The vast majority of human memory is narrowly focused and oblivious to what it has missed. In like fashion, every choice that a historian makes to emphasize a particular story, figure, or detail is a neglect of many others in the periphery. This is just how memory works and history, of course, mimics memory. Forgetfulness is the rule; memory is the exception. So we can only take the neglect of ancient historians and narratives so far.

Modern investigators do their best to observe the proverbial smoke that betrays the fire, but we must be willing to acknowledge when there is no smoke to behold. Concerning a possible wife of Jesus, it is necessary to point out the rules of androcentric history. In doing so, we simply open the door to a historical possibility. Silence does not prove that Jesus was celibate. It also does not prove that he was married.

CHALLENGES

Any discussion of a possible wife of Jesus must contend with the problem of silence. First, the names and voices of women tend to be obscured by ancient and modern historians. Second, we see this very tendency in our sources for the life of Jesus. We have every reason to believe that James, the brother of Jesus, was married. Is the silence that obscures James' wife the same sort of silence that we might expect to render a wife of Jesus inaudible?

In the case of Salome, I have pointed to a tendency to take liberties with her silence. Many who have fictionalized her appended their own ideologies onto her name. To some extent, historians and novelists cannot help but to exploit the unknown. This is not necessarily a bad thing; we must retell our important stories with creativity in order to save them. But we must be self-aware as we do so. If not held in check, our imaginations can do violence to the very figure we hope to commemorate.

FURTHER READING

Markus Bockmuehl, *Simon Peter in Scripture and Memory: The New Testament Apostle in the Early Church* (Grand Rapids: Baker Academic, 2012).

Bart Ehrman, *Lost Christianities: The Battles for Scripture and the Faiths We Never Knew* (Oxford: Oxford University Press, 2005).

Anne Lapidus Lerner, *Eternally Eve: Images of Eve in the Hebrew Bible* (Lebanon, NH: Brandeis University Press, 2007).

Amy-Jill Levine with Maria Mayo Robbins, *A Feminist Companion to the New Testament Apocrypha: Feminist Companion to the New Testament and Early Christian Writings* (Cleveland: Pilgrim Press, 2006).

Christopher W. Skinner, *What Are They Saying About the Gospel of Thomas?* (Mahwah, NJ: Paulist Press, 2012).

Something about Mary

"Greet one another with a holy kiss."
– SAINT PAUL

Almost two thousand years after Mary Magdalene's death, she has become the subject of a modern scandal. Our earliest accounts of Mary say that she had seven demons cast out of her, that she pursued an education normally reserved for men, and that she witnessed a dead man come back to life. These are all incredible claims. What is less incredible, by far, is the statement that she might have been married.

Given the choice of (a) demon-possessed, (b) shattered gender stereotypes, (c) witnessed a resurrection, or (d) was married, which of these topics is most likely to inspire a Hollywood film? Interestingly, the answer is (d). Ron Howard's 2006 film adaptation of *The Da Vinci Code* grossed over $758 million worldwide. The story was inspired by the premise that Mary Magdalene was indeed married and that her descendants survive today.

Of course, it wasn't the fact that she might have wed but *who* she might have wed that made the book and the film controversial. In 1988, Martin Scorsese's film adaptation of *The Last Temptation of Christ* created controversy by suggesting that Jesus was sexually attracted to Mary. Mary has become controversial because of the possible window that she provides into Jesus' sexuality.

FASCINATION AND JEALOUSY

An important voice on the topic of Mary Magdalene's evolution in Christian thought belongs to April DeConick, a scholar of early Christianity. One of the prominent threads of DeConick's *Holy Misogyny* is the story of the erasure of women from Christian origins. She demonstrates how Mary Magdalene was initially remembered as a key figure among the earliest Christians, only to be systematically diminished in the mid-to late first century: "Jesus appears to have been something of a woman's advocate during his era, and women were present in his mission as patrons and disciples."[1] But the institutionalization of Christianity would not treat the memory of Mary kindly.

Tragically, we only see snippets of Mary's life; fortunately, we see enough to be convinced that she was an important figure among the first apostles. It seems that her story was simply too fascinating to be eclipsed entirely. What happens when a figure is almost entirely forgotten by historical record but too compelling to ignore? As we saw with Salome: *imagination fills in the gaps.* Without a doubt,

---

THE NAG HAMMADI LIBRARY

Nag Hammadi Library is a collection of Coptic texts unearthed in 1945 in Upper Egypt. Several gospels that are not found in the New Testament were discovered in this collection, including the *Gospel of Thomas*, the *Gospel of Philip*, the *Gospel of the Egyptians*, and many others. These texts represent versions of Christianity that were prominent in the second century onward but were eventually branded heretical by the apostolic church.

---

second-century Christian imagination and modern historical fiction have this in common.

In recent decades, several fragments of "gospels" have been uncovered that feature Mary Magdalene prominently. These, as you might guess, are not found in the New Testament. What scholars refer to as the Nag Hammadi Library reveals the impact that Mary Magdalene had on early Christian imagination. One of the key themes, where Magdalene is concerned, is the jealousy that she provoked in Jesus' male disciples.

One text that features this theme prominently is called the *Gospel of Philip*, composed about one hundred years (or more) after Mary Magdalene was dead and gone. It is a collection of loosely related reflections about what it means to be spiritually enlightened. As with the four Gospels found in the Christian Bible, the key theme of this book is the worship of Jesus. But unlike Matthew, Mark, Luke, and John, the *Gospel of Philip* gives us almost no information about events in the life of Jesus.

What has made *Philip* famous in recent years is what it claims about Mary Magdalene. *Philip* tells us that Mary Magdalene was the "lover" of Jesus and that he "loved her more than all the disciples, and used to kiss her often on her mouth." Of course, this detail allows the author to extend the jealousy theme. The male disciples ask, "Why do you love her more than all of us?"[2]

From a modern perspective, it is almost impossible to resist taking this at face value. A plain sense reading of this text would seem to indicate that Jesus and Mary were physically intimate. The trouble with reading it in this way is that *Philip* is not a "plain sense" sort of document. In fact, one of the unique features of *Philip* is elitism. What really mattered to the group and to the author who composed *Philip* was hidden meaning and enlightenment that transcended common sense.

Philip also claims that there were three Marys linked to Jesus. Mary was Jesus' "sister, mother, and lover."[3] The name Mary seems to be symbolic in this text. Mary represents the ideal disciple. In fact, here is what *Philip* says about being plain-spoken:

> The words we give to earthly realities engender illusion, they turn the heart away from the real to the unreal . . . words do not speak reality . . . all the words we hear in this world only deceive us . . . The Truth makes use of the words in the world because without these words, it would remain totally unknowable. The Truth is one and many, so as to teach us the innumerable One of Love.[4]

The school of thought that produced the *Gospel of Philip* believed that words were unable to capture reality. The words "mother, sister, and lover" were symbols that transcended common meaning. If we were to take these words literally, this author would probably accuse us of being "unworthy of life." You really don't get more elitist than that. Bart Ehrman explains that books such as *Philip* "are for insiders who – unlike us – already have all the background information they need."[5] Really, nothing in the *Gospel of Philip* was intended to be taken at face value.

Most scholars think that the author of *Philip* belonged to a Christian sect called the "Valentinians."[6] While "mainstream" Christianity (that which we commemorate as "apostolic" Christianity) taught that the death and resurrection of Christ would bring salvation, Valentinus believed that Jesus taught his true disciples the mysteries of heaven, and that the knowledge of this truth would bring salvation.[7] One characteristic of this particular group is that they were keenly interested in sexual symbolism. Unlike many Christian groups who held serious misgivings about female participation in worship, the Valentinians believed that the male–female union was essential for enlightenment.[8]

A POSSIBLE RECONSTRUCTION OF
VALENTINIAN THEOLOGY

In order to describe how a singular God could create such a diverse world, the Valentinians imagined that God the Father projected thought and that this thought took the form of "Intellect" (male) and "Truth" (female). This pair of personalities produced another pair of male and female counterparts, and that pair produced another, and so on. Each pair was one step removed from God the Father, but all of these existed within the mind of God. Importantly, each pair was a masculine and feminine union. But one of the lowest projections was a feminine form called "Wisdom." She severed herself from her male counterpart and attempted to gain direct knowledge of God. This ruined the harmonious balance of the cosmos, and it was this misinformed personality that created the material world. The *Gospel of Philip* says that: "The world came into being through an error."[9] For the Valentinians, marriage between male and female was a way to correct the corruption of the material world.

Because of the Valentinians' fondness for symbol, mystery, and metaphor, it is difficult to tell how much of their sex talk represents practice. Many scholars think that the Valentinians were all talk, that they used sexual metaphor to describe their spiritual ecstasy. Others believe that spiritual ecstasy was achieved through physical enactment. In this view, coitus, when performed by an enlightened married couple in sacred ritual, was a symbol of divine unity. DeConick explains: "The highest aspiration for the Valentinians was the marriage of purity, a conjugal relationship that was defined by sexual behavior with a spiritual focus."[10]

In either case, Mary became a symbolic exemplar for this group. The Valentinians believed that physical gender was not indicative of the collective gender of the human race. They believed that all human spirits were female. Humans are female elements that derive from masculine (angelic) counterparts. In this view, humans will continue to be alienated from the mind of God until they are united with their higher, masculine selves at the end of time. But in the interim, union could be enacted through a "baptism of light." From this perspective, Mary was able to achieve her true self through union with Jesus and became an example for all disciples (male and female).

It is highly likely that the group responsible for the *Gospel of Philip* is talking about a different kind of "kissing." From their perspective, kissing probably symbolized their ongoing transformation into spiritual being. This symbol might have been borrowed from other sacred narratives where a spiritually superior being would breathe life into a person to bring them to life, sometimes eternal life.

We may see this idea reflected in a story about God and Adam. Genesis tells us that "the Lord God formed man from the dust of the ground, and breathed into his nostrils the breath of life; and the man became a living being."[11] We probably see something close to this sort of special breathing at the end of John's Gospel: "Jesus said to them again, 'Peace be with you. As the Father has sent me, so I send you.' When he had said this, he breathed on them and said to them, 'Receive the Holy Spirit.'"[12] The *Gospel of Thomas* has a different spin on this: "Jesus says: 'He who drinks from my mouth will become like me. As for me, I will become what he is, and what is hidden will be revealed to him.'"[13]

With this in mind, consider this passage from *Philip*:

> All of those who are begotten in the world are begotten by physical means; the others are begotten by spiritual means. Those who are begotten by the spirit hope for the realization of humanity ... The realized human is fertilized by a kiss, and is born through a kiss. This is why we kiss each other, giving birth to each other through the grace that is in us.[14]

If the larger esoteric portrait of *Philip* is brought into view, "kissing" seems to have been a ritual to extend the breath of life (from Jesus) from one living soul to the next. This imaginative portrait of Mary illustrated how a disciple could attain unity with God. It was this sort of spiritual intimacy that made the imagined male apostles jealous.

PROBLEMS WITH PHILIP

There is one further wrinkle to consider before we move behind the *Gospel of Philip*'s portraits of Jesus and Mary and attempt to say anything about these figures historically. Like many ancient documents from the period, the text quoted above is fragmented. Time and nature have eaten away some of the *Gospel of Philip* so that the passage in question looks like this when literally translated: " ... and ... companion of the ... Mary Magdalene ... used to ... more than the disciples ... kiss her ... times the rest ..." These gaps in the text represent places where the document has worn away. Coptic scholars are in the business of filling in these sorts of gaps, but the fragmentary state of this passage should give us reason for caution: "Our curiosity notwithstanding, we simply cannot know what was in the gaps."[15] There is enough information, however, to warrant some discussion about the nature of "kissing" in this context.[16]

But the real problem with the *Gospel of Philip* is this: what makes Philip's statement about Mary scandalous for us is not what would have made it scandalous to the first audiences of this gospel. We read that Jesus "used to kiss her often on her mouth," and we think of this as a keyhole look into Jesus' libido. It sounds like schoolboy gossip to us. But to most of its ancient audiences, *Philip's* portrait of Mary would have scandalized for a different reason entirely. A major question among many Christians was this: *Are women (as inferior beings) worthy to receive eternal life?* Even more shocking to these audiences: *If Jesus gave a larger portion of his breath to Mary, does this mean that Peter and the other male disciples are inferior?*

THE GOSPEL OF MARY

This gospel was probably composed in the second century and survives only in a few fragments. While most scholars hold to this date, Harvard professor Karen King has suggested a much earlier date. The least fragmentary of these is a fifth-century Coptic text. This text was purchased by a German scholar named Carl Reinhardt from an unknown manuscript dealer in Cairo in 1896. Two earlier (third-century) Greek fragments were discovered shortly thereafter.

According to *Mary*, the post-resurrection Jesus taught his disciples (both male and female) before his ultimate departure to Heaven. After grieving his departure, the male disciples ask Mary Magdalene to tell them what Jesus taught her privately. It seems that Jesus revealed otherwise secret teaching to Mary in a vision. Mary describes this vision. However, much of this vision has been lost due to the fragmentary nature of the document.

So, while we are preoccupied with sexuality, they were preoccupied with spiritual hierarchy. It is Mary Magdalene's spiritual status and not her sex life that would have made her a scandalous figure in this context. Hierarchy in the spiritual realm is a key theme

Saint Mary Magdalene (c. 1520), Quinten Matsys. This oil painting is more subtle than most depictions of Mary Magdalene. Here she is sober and not overtly sexualized. However, the alabaster jar is a common indicator that the nameless woman of Luke 7:37–39 is associated with Mary Magdalene. In that text, the nameless woman with an alabaster jar full of ointment washes and anoints Jesus' feet. She is called a "sinner" in the narrative. Thus Matsys' "Saint" betrays her legacy in Christian love as a sinner.

in the *Gospel of Mary*. In this text, as we would expect, Peter and the other male disciples are jealous of Mary. Again, the scandal is that Mary's access to spiritual enlightenment is beyond what a misogynist might expect from a woman.

The *Gospel of Thomas* (the last verse of this gospel) conveys this exchange between Peter and Jesus concerning Mary: "Simon Peter said to them, 'Mary should leave us, for females are not worthy of life.' Jesus said, 'See, I am going to attract her to make her male so that she too might become a living spirit that resembles you males. For every female thing that makes itself male will enter the kingdom of heaven.'"[17] This saying may seem bizarre and offensive to our ears, but it demonstrates that the scandal of feminine spirituality was a hot topic for some early Christians. This passage has been notoriously puzzling for scholars of *Thomas*. But among some early Christians, the move to make Mary "male" might have been seen as a way to link Mary to her spiritual masculinity. Could this be what was at stake in Philip's description of Jesus and Mary "kissing"?

KISSING IN FIRST-CENTURY CHRISTIANITY?

So far I have argued that the *Gospel of Philip* (alongside a handful of other second to fourth-century gospels) represents an imaginative reconstruction of Mary Magdalene. But it is important to recognize that historical imagination is not conjured from thin air. The gnostic imagination was fertile insomuch as Jesus fit into their unique mythology of creation, demigods, and souls entrapped within an evil material world. At the same time, these imaginative stories were loosely related to conversations about Jesus that began in the first century.

The obvious next step, then, is to ask: Does the *Gospel of Philip* reflect a memory of Jesus and Mary that began among Jesus' contemporaries? The most common answer given by historical Jesus scholars is to say "almost not at all." The gnostic teachings of Jesus are inventions of gnostic Christianity. Some scholars will grant that the jealousy of Mary expressed by the male disciples reflects late first-century disputes about women in Christian leadership, but what of the kissing?

As surprising as it might sound, there is a strong possibility that kissing was a common practice among many early Christians. In Jesus' world, kissing was an intimate greeting reserved for family members.[18] In fact, there are at least five (maybe six) instances of this sort of kissing in the New Testament. This practice fits well with Christianity's belief that their religious group formed a spiritual family.[19] As seen in the quotation that began this chapter, Paul encourages intimacy and solidarity among Christians symbolized by a "holy kiss."

There is no doubt that the *Gospel of Philip*'s understanding of the holy kiss took on new meaning, but the author didn't invent the practice. We can safely say that the early Christians kissed like brothers and sisters. What we do not see in the earliest Christian documents is the holy kiss taking on erotic significance. New Testament scholar Paul Foster aptly summarizes that in Jesus' culture, familial kisses "did not carry the same overtones that have become attached to this practice in a highly sexualized modern society."[20] The *Gospel of Philip* claims that Mary was Jesus' "sister, mother, and lover." As long as we keep in mind that these are metaphors for spiritual intimacy, we can indeed affirm that the *Gospel of Philip* reflects early Christian memory.

Did Jesus kiss Mary often on the mouth? While it is not unimaginable, we really cannot affirm or deny this claim with any confidence. The best evidence we have that Jesus practiced the holy kiss with his disciples comes from the story of his betrayal. In dramatic irony,

Judas greets Jesus with a kiss, a symbol of intimacy and solidarity; the gesture results in Jesus' arrest and execution. Does this episode suggest the practice of an ancient ritual that stems from Jesus' teachings? The question will have to be left open.

CHALLENGES

What we can say with confidence is that there were women disciples in Jesus' following. Mary Magdalene was prominent within this group. The memory of Mary's inclusion remained a talking point among Christians for decades and centuries after. Indeed, she was probably remarkable among the diciples and too intriguing not to attract imaginative reconstructions of her relationship with Jesus.

The recent move to impregnate Mary Magdalene with sexual scandal belittles her historical significance. She wasn't simply the nameless "wife" or "mother" or "sister" of someone. She transcended these categories. In Valentinian imagination, Mary was the ideal disciple, transformed by her relationship with Jesus. This belief may well reflect early historical memory. Mary was probably considered a "disciple." If so, she transcended the common ranks of beast, female, male, enlightened male, deity. Mary found union with Christ. Mary is a symbol for all disciples (male and female) who find union with their higher, spiritual selves. Mary is the example of a human who has been saved from alienation and restored to harmony within the structure of the cosmos.

What we do not find in these portraits is a Mary Magdalene who was the literal wife of Jesus. Given the Valentinian philosophy about "literal" descriptions of reality, a literal wife of Jesus is the last thing that we would expect from them. This should be kept in mind when reading the next chapter, where I discuss how Mary's fictional persona devolved the popular imagination.

FURTHER READING

David Brakke, *The Gnostics: Myth, Ritual, and Diversity in Early Christianity* (Cambridge: Harvard University Press, 2010).

April D. DeConick, *The Original Gospel of Thomas in Translation: With a Commentary and New English Translation of the Complete Gospel: Library of New Testament Studies* (London: T & T Clark, 2007).

April D. DeConick, *Holy Misogyny: Why the Sex and Gender Conflicts in the Early Church Still Matter* (New York: Continuum, 2011).

Karen L. King, *The Gospel of Mary of Magdala: Jesus and the First Woman Apostle* (Santa Rosa: Poleridge Press, 2003).

Richard Valantasis, *The Gospel of Thomas: New Testament Readings* (New York: Routledge, 1997).

MRS. CHRIST

"No other biblical figure – including Judas and perhaps even Jesus – has had such a vivid and bizarre post-biblical life in the human imagination, in legend, and in art."

– JANE SCHABERG

The topic of Jesus' sexuality has traditionally been taboo. But those who have ventured to explore it have demonstrated a variously "normal" Jesus. Whether Jesus is struggling with his desires, as in Nikos Kazantzakis's novel *The Last Temptation of Christ*[1] (on which the Scorsese film is based), or he is married with children as with Dan Brown's portrait, or he is sacrificially celibate as with John P. Meier's portrait,[2] the Jesus that scandalizes us is (most often) a man who embodies the sexual norms of the Christianized West. Dale B. Martin writes: "I have no interest in arguing for any of these different proposals for Jesus' sexuality. I find certain assumptions undergirding each of them difficult to accept. What is more interesting for my purposes is how they illustrate what has been imaginable at different times with regard to the sexuality of Jesus – and what has been apparently unimaginable."[3] Martin's point offers us a way forward. We can learn much about a culture from that culture's collective imagination. We can also learn a great deal about a culture from its imaginative limits.

In this chapter, I will sketch the story of how Mary Magdalene became imaginable as the wife of Jesus. I will survey her emergence as "the sinful woman" and show how, in the imaginations of medieval Christianity, she eventually became a prostitute. I will then speak to Mary's very recent transformation from wanton to wife.

MAGDALENE IN POPULAR IMAGINATION

In 591, Pope Gregory I declares (and thus lends official authority to) what was probably a common belief: that Mary Magdalene, Mary the sister of Martha and Lazarus, and the nameless "sinner" who washed and kissed the feet of Jesus in Luke 7, were the same person. Gregory believes that she is "the woman John calls Mary, and that Mary from whom Mark says seven demons were cast out. And what did these seven devils signify, if not all the vices?"

Although the New Testament does not specify that these three women are the same person, Gregory creatively conflates them.[4] In doing so, he transforms Mary into a sinner and infuses her legacy with scandal:

> It is clear, brothers, that the woman previously used the unguent to perfume her flesh in forbidden acts. What she therefore displayed more scandalously, she was not offering to God in a more praiseworthy manner. She had coveted with earthly eyes, but now through penitence these are consumed with tears. She displayed her hair to set off her face, but now her hair dries her tears. She had spoken proud things with her mouth, but in kissing the Lord's feet, she now planted her mouth on the Redeemer's feet. For every delight, therefore, she had had in herself, she now immolated herself. She turned the mass of crimes to virtues, in order to serve God entirely in penance, for as much as she had wrongly held God in contempt.[5]

Gregory paints a portrait of a woman who once perfumed "her flesh in forbidden acts" but became repentant at the feet of Jesus.

This image of a sinful woman turned virtuously submissive dominated Catholic commemoration of Magdalene for the next fourteen centuries.[6]

In 1260 an archbishop named Jacobus de Voragine wrote a historical fiction of Magdalene's life where he repeats Gregory's merger of Mary of Bethany and Mary Magdalene. Jacobus also imagines how she might have fallen into prostitution:

> She was wellborn, descended of royal stock. Her father's name was Syrus, her mother was called Eucharia. With her brother Lazarus and her sister Martha, she owned Magdalum, a walled town two miles from Genezareth, along Bethany, not far from Jerusalem, and a considerable part of Jerusalem itself . . . Magdalene, then, was very rich, and sensuous pleasure keeps company with great wealth. Renown as she was for her beauty and her riches, she was no less known for the way she gave her body to pleasure – so much so that her proper name was forgotten and she was commonly called "the sinner."[7]

Jacobus exploits the name of Mary's village (thought to be "Magdala") and portrays her as a wealthy, indeed royal, woman of a great city. He then describes how her wealth gave way to sensuous pleasures. Jacobus renders her explicitly – if implausibly – as a prostitute. He also mimics the standard image of Mary as a repentant sinner.

The portrait of Mary's repentance became important during the Protestant Reformation. In 1566, Bishop Hugh Latimer said this in a sermon: "I doubt not we all be Magdalenes in falling into sin and in offending: but we be not again Magdalenes in knowing ourselves and rising from sin."[8] Here Mary becomes a model for the Christian life. Latimer's Magdalene represents all of humanity, steeped in sin, but redeemed by grace. In Latimer's sermon we see no attempt to merge the lives of the tearful woman of Luke 7, and the woman who witnessed the resurrection in Mark, chapter sixteen. That Mary was the sinner *par excellence* is simply assumed.

But the Reformation made readers out of many, and countless non-clergy began to read the Bible. An interesting example of this comes from the pen of the poet John Donne (1572–1631). Donne demonstrates that not everyone swallowed Gregory's portrait of Mary:

> Her of your name, whose fair inheritance
> Bethina was, and jointure Magdalo:
> An active faith so highly did advance,
> That she once knew, more than the Church did know,
> The Resurrection; so much good there is
> Deliver'd of her, that some Fathers be
> Loth to believe one Woman could do this;
> But, think these Magdalens were two or three.[9]

Here Donne demonstrates that some "Fathers" believed that there were multiple women represented in the stories that Gregory conflated. Notice, however, that Donne maintains the Bethany connection and imagines that Mary was wealthy. English literature scholar Alison Chapman is probably correct to think that Donne has borrowed from Jacobus's portrayal of Mary as a wealthy woman but omits her descent into prostitution.[10]

Jacobus's portrait eventually found its way to the silver screen. In Cecil B. DeMille's 1927 *King of Kings,* "Mary of Magdala" is a wealthy socialite. The second frame of the movie reads: "In Judea – groaning under the iron heel of Rome – the beautiful courtesan, MARY of MAGDALA, laughed alike at God and Man."[11] Mary petulantly orders her servants to fetch her perfume. She travels by way of chariot driven by zebras (a gift from the Nubian King). At one point she grabs a male guest by the throat and pins him down, demanding information from him. Even so, her portrait is sexualized as she entertains several wealthy men who flirt with her and beg her for kisses. When she eventually meets Jesus, he casts out her demons, the first of which is Lust. After the exorcism is complete, Mary covers herself to convey her new spirit of diminutive modesty and kneels to wash the feet of a radiant Jesus.

Thus the image of Mary as a wealthy, but sex-driven woman continued into the modern era. The description of Mary as a "courtesan" hints at the modern usage of the word as "prostitute" but casts her in a Renaissance-style role as a "woman at court." So Mary Magdalene's image as a reformed prostitute, while cleverly disguised in DeMille's film, is given homage. Indeed, Mary's portrait as a reformed prostitute continues to dominate her commemoration in the Christianized West.

In 1945, the unearthing of the Nag Hammadi Library would change Mary's popular image dramatically. The *Gospel of Philip* (as discussed in the previous chapter) suggested the possibility that Jesus and Mary were lovers, or at least that some third-century mystics played with this metaphor. Shortly after these gospels were found, the novelist, philosopher, and politician Nikos Kazantzakis published his novel *The Last Temptation of Christ.*

In this historical fiction, Mary's life as a prostitute is central to the plot. Jesus is attracted to her and struggles with his desires for sexual gratification and for marital normalcy. In this "dream," Jesus imagines himself married to Magdalene, who soon becomes pregnant. Soon after, Mary dies and Jesus' dream of a family is shattered. Jesus then settles down with Mary and Martha to start a family. Thus Kazantzakis does not make the mistake of merging Mary Magdalene and Mary of Bethany. Martin Scorsese's film adaption of the book repeats this portrait.[12]

In one scene, toward the beginning of the film, Jesus sheepishly enters Mary's brothel and watches her having sex with multiple clients. The screenplay reads:

> Besides the young Indian nobleman (with three gold bands around his ankles), there are three Bedouin, three old men with painted eyelashes and nails, two young men with black beards and moustaches, and two rich black merchants. An old lady is off to one side crouched on the ground with a small cage containing some crabs. A small fire is beside her on which she is cooking food. There is no door to Magdalene's room where she does business, only a wispy half torn curtain floating in the infrequent breeze. This affords her waiting clients a half-darkened view of the proceedings. An Arab makes love to her. She is nude, and good at her work.[13]

Played by actor Willem Dafoe, this Jesus waits and watches and then struggles to ask for Mary's forgiveness. Mary is hostile to Jesus' false piety and accuses him of hypocrisy. Jesus tells her, "God can save your soul." Mary replies, "I don't want him. He's already broken my heart." In this portrait, Mary sounds like a modern woman who has lost her faith. In contrast, Jesus is a tortured soul, struggling with his sexual desires and trying to purge them.

Both characters develop toward redemption as Jesus begins his mission. Jesus' sin thereafter – his last temptation – is experienced in his imagination as he struggles with his vocation as the messiah. Mary's repentance is imagined differently than Jacobus de Voragine's medieval portrait, but she still moves from prostitute to follower of Jesus.

The scandal that surrounded *The Last Temptation of Christ* keyed on Jesus' imaginary hope for a life of normalcy. Christians, in particular, boycotted the film and attempted to ban the book because the thought of Jesus' sexual imagination was sacrilegious.[14] Very little of the media coverage was devoted to questioning Mary's sexualized portrait. Few, it seems, had a problem with Mary's portrait as a prostitute. This assumption was so ingrained in the popular imagination of the Christianized West that Mary's prostitution was uncontroversial.

In the mid-1990s the Dave Matthews Band was one of the most internationally recognized rock groups. At the height of their popularity, the band put out an acoustic song titled "Christmas Song."[15] The song's message and common refrain framed the life of Jesus in "love, love, love." Love is "all around" is repeated in successive stages of Jesus' life. The song begins by labelling Mary and Joseph boyfriend and girlfriend. The wise men come to shower the new baby with love. When Jesus grows up he meets another Mary who is of ill repute. Moreover, this Mary is willing to sell her reputation for a reasonable fee. And yet, Jesus' heart is full of love for Mary. This song reinforces Mary's popular depiction as a prostitute. The song suggests – not so subtly – that this less-than-reputable Mary was Jesus' lover. Here we see that the image of Mary Magdalene the repentant sinner has been eclipsed by Mary the prostitute turned lover. But the song also shows how successful Kazantzakis was. Less subtle is a fictional exchange between Stephen King's "gunslinger" and a priest. The gunslinger asks if Jesus was ever married. The priest retorts, "No… but His girlfriend was a whore." While Magdalene is not named, King's fictional priest confirms a popular reading of her legacy.[16]

Other seeds of change in Mary's public persona are seen in a poem by Veronica Patterson. Patterson's poem is titled "I Want to Say Your Name: *a love poem.*"[17] The subtitle is crucial to understanding what follows. The poem begins in the first person; the poet's voice calling to a lover. The poet wants to say the lover's name "the way Jesus said 'Mary.'" In this way, the poet is drawing a parallel between Mary and Jesus and two modern lovers. Mary stands with Jesus at the open tomb after Jesus has resurrected from the grave. She wants to touch him but he tells her that she cannot. Jesus is in between death and life, the physical and spiritual, and he cannot accept physical affection. Still the poet creates a palpable tension between Jesus and Mary. The poem climaxes with a simple and profound intimacy:

> "Mary," he said, and she changed, as if
> an hour earlier she had been a child, Her name
> held all of her and it was his gift.

In Patterson's poem – called "a love poem" – Mary is intimately known. There is no mistaking her identity; "Her name held all of her" and Jesus knew her. Moreover, the imagined setting returns us to the empty tomb of Jesus: the place where Mary Magdalene is most associated in the four biblical Gospels. This is not the prostitute, the sinner, or the sister of Martha. The intimacy between Mary and Jesus has eclipsed all else. But, like Donne's poem, Patterson's imagination is exceptional. It doesn't represent the more popular image of Mary the prostitute.

Remarkably, it wasn't until Dan Brown's massively popular novel that the general public began to imagine a Mary devoid of prostitution. The idea that she was Jesus' lover was fascinating, but the proposal that she was the wife of Jesus was a runaway hit. In Brown's detective mystery, a modern French woman named Sophie learns of an ancient cover-up concerning the marriage of Jesus and Mary. According to the story, this secret "history" has been communicated through the work of Renaissance artist Leonardo Da Vinci. Brown writes:

> Sophie moved closer to the image [of Da Vinci's *Last Supper*]. The woman to Jesus' right was young and pious-looking, with a demure face, beautiful red hair, and hands folded quietly. *This is the woman who singlehandedly could crumble the Church?*
> "Who is she?" Sophie asked.
> "That, my dear," Teabing replied, "is Mary Magdalene."
> Sophie turned. "The prostitute?"

> Teabing drew a short breath, as if the word had injured him
> personally. "Magdalene was no such thing. That unfortunate
> misconception is the legacy of a smear campaign launched by
> the early Church."[18]

This portrait of Magdalene as the secret wife of Jesus was too compelling to ignore, and just scandalous enough to turn a fun detective novel into an international debate. The novel dominated the *New York Times* bestsellers list for over two years (2003–05) and was boycotted by many churches when it was made into a film. Multiple books by Christian scholars and apologists were published for the sole purpose of exposing the historical inaccuracies of the book.

But for all of the book's fictive elements (it was fiction, after all), Dan Brown probably did the most to expose Gregory's fallacy to the general public. The fictitious Mary of *The Da Vinci Code* was not a prostitute. Brown's Mary was, however, royalty. A key element to the plotline was that both Mary and Jesus were of royal lineage.[19] This, of course, recalls the historical fiction by Jacobus in the thirteenth century. Brown discarded what he did not like of the medieval historical fiction and kept what would most help his plot. Ironically, his fiction undermined the fictitious image of Mary as a prostitute.

There are now two competing images of Mary in the popular imagination of the Christianized West. The first is Mary the prostitute; the second is Mary the wife of Jesus. The former can be traced to the Middle Ages, and the latter has emerged as a contender only in recent years.

THE *GOSPEL OF JESUS' WIFE*

In September 2012, the International Congress of Coptic Studies was hosted in Rome. At this conference, a well-respected Harvard scholar, Karen King, announced that an anonymous collector had produced an ancient fragment that looked to be a fourth-century fragment of a second-century gospel. King titled this fragment the *Gospel of Jesus' Wife*. This small piece of papyrus contains a few Coptic phrases that caused an immediate media frenzy. Translated, the entire fragment reads:[20]

Side One:

1] "not [to] me. My mother gave to me li[fe ... "
2] The disciples said to Jesus, ".[
3] deny. Mary is worthy of it [
4] ... " Jesus said to them, "My wife .[
5] ... she will be able to be my disciple ... [
6] Let wicked people swell up ... [
7] As for me, I dwell with her in order to . [
8] an image [

Side Two:

1] my moth[er
2] three [
3] ... [
4] forth which ... [
5] (illegible ink traces)
6] (illegible ink traces)

As you can see, this gospel is little more than a few disjointed phrases. Among these phrases, quite clearly, is the phrase "my wife." Coupled with the phrase "I dwell with her," this document offers evidence that the author linked Jesus and Mary together as husband and wife. If this fragment is ancient, it would be the first reference to a literal wife of Jesus. Recalling my previous discussion of the *Gospel of Philip*, some had imagined Mary as the "lover" of Jesus, but not specifically as his wife.

The paper by King was published on the Harvard webpage and provisionally accepted by the *Harvard Theological Review*. At least two experts (papyrologists) who were consulted before the announcement were relatively convinced that the document was authentic. But King was also alerted to the fact that one of the reviewers pointed to several problems with the fragment, suggesting that it was a modern forgery. Within a week of this announcement, several other scholars went on the record arguing that it was a fraud. In the months that followed, the scholarly consensus leaned more and more toward forgery.

New Testament scholar Francis Watson writes: "The text has been constructed out of small pieces – words or phrases – culled from the Coptic *Gospel of Thomas* . . . and set in new contexts. This is most probably the compositional procedure of a modern author who is not a native speaker of Coptic."[21] Many others, agreeing with Watson, pointed out that the phrases culled from the *Gospel of Thomas* provided just the right amount of information to scandalize the general public.

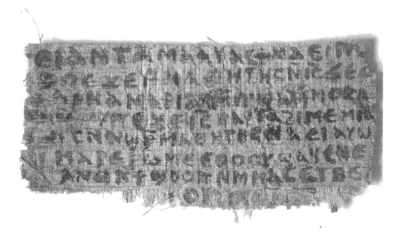

"The Gospel of Jesus' Wife" so named by Professor Karen King. This fragment of papyrus is approximately 1.5 by 3 inches.

Among the many arguments for forgery is an intriguing suggestion from Oxford-educated researcher Andrew Bernhard.[22] Bernhard observes that every phrase[23] in the *Gospel of Jesus' Wife* could have been stolen from an online Coptic-English resource called an "interlinear."[24] Interlinears are used by students as translation aids. As seen in the example below, the English translation is typically set in between the lines of the ancient text.

What I provide here shows that the exact phrase found in *the Gospel of Jesus' Wife* is present in the Coptic *Gospel of Thomas*. Both texts contain the phrase "my mother gave me life."

50:01/608	[ЄВ]Оλ	[ТΛ·МλλY]	ΔЄ	М̄·МЄ	λС·†	NλЄI	·П·ШN2	27
	forth;	my-mother,	hwvr,	true,	she-gave	to-me	The-Life.	
50:02/609	ПЄХЄ·ІС	[ХЄ	О]YОЄІ	NλY	М·ФλРІСλІОС	ХЄ		28
102*	*Said-*JS89*	this:	Woe	to-them,	the-Pharisees,	for		

It just so happens that this particular online text contains a typo. It leaves out a prefix, a definite object marker that looks like $\overline{M}$. I have enlarged the problematic portion here:

$$\overline{M}$$
λС·†   NλЄI   ·П·ШN2
she-gave   to-me   The-Life.

This oddity is not found in any ancient manuscript related to Christianity. It is unique to this modern reproduction that has been available online since 1997. In fact, this typo has been corrected in other online versions of the *Gospel of Thomas*. But the *Gospel of Jesus' Wife* contains the same oddity:

I have shown here where the prefix should have been. Again, this oddity can *only* be found in the online interlinear shown above. Let me put this as bluntly as I can: if Bernhard is correct, the author of this document had an internet connection. If so, it is a *very* modern forgery.

What is more interesting to me is the timing of this discovery and the media coverage that exploded when it was announced. Whether authentic or not, the news media's coverage of this text reveals a great deal about Mary's newly minted image. Despite King's clear and repeated efforts to the contrary, the international news media sold this story as if it might reveal something about the historical Jesus. In the first paragraph of King's paper, she writes: "This is the only extant ancient text which explicitly portrays Jesus as referring to a wife. It does not, however, provide evidence that the historical Jesus was married, given the late date of the fragment and the probable date of original composition only in the second half of the second century."

This is an important statement because the story that circulated on the blogosphere, on the evening news, and on several comedy programs assumed that this gospel was published to say something scandalous about Jesus himself. Clearly, King had hoped to contribute to the discussion about second-century Christianity, not historical Jesus research. A journalist for the *New York Times*, Laurie Goodstein, wrote one of the first articles about King's fragment: "[King] repeatedly cautioned that this fragment should not be taken as proof that Jesus, the historical person, was actually married. The text was probably written centuries after Jesus lived, and all other early, historically reliable Christian literature is silent on the question."

But in the same article, Goodstein also wrote: "Even with many questions unsettled, the discovery could reignite the debate over whether Jesus was married, whether Mary Magdalene was his wife and whether he had a female disciple. These debates date to the early centuries of Christianity, scholars say. But they are relevant today, when global Christianity is roiling over the place of women in ministry and the boundaries of marriage."[25]

Seemingly, this paragraph is an invitation to us, the readers, to reconsider our own "roiling" debates. Like many other innovations to the popular image of Mary, our own concerns drive our collective imaginings of Mary. It matters very little whether or not Mary was Jesus' wife. What makes this fragment relevant, according to Goodstein, is the opportunity it creates for us to continue the cultural debates that are already under way.

Notice the way that Reuters' journalist Philip Pullella frames this discovery: "The idea that Jesus was married resurfaces regularly in popular culture, notably with the 2003 publication of Dan Brown's best-seller 'The Da Vinci Code,' which angered the Vatican because it was based on the idea that Jesus was married to Mary Magdalene and had children."[26]

In order to tap into (and fuel) the popular imaginations of the general public, Pullella invites his readers to remember the controversies stirred by Dan Brown's fiction. Undoubtedly, it is the Mary Magdalene of *fiction* that guides our collective imagination and allows us to focus our agendas. Even when discussing ancient possibilities, it is near impossible to keep our popular portraits of Mary and Jesus in the realm of the imagination.

With this in mind, I will point out the obvious: as compared to the two-thousand-year history of popular portraits of Mary Magdalene, the notion that she was literally married to Jesus is ten years young. The seeds were planted in our imagination by the discovery of the *Gospel of Philip*. Mary was sensationalized by Kazantzakis's Jesus, who *imagined* himself as a married man. But the image of Mary as the *literal* wife of Jesus was novel in 2003. Could it be that the *Gospel of Jesus' Wife* fragment emerged specifically to fan the controversies specific to the third millennium?

We should expect our popular images of Mary Magdalene to embody our social debates and agendas. Judging from the way that the various news outlets reported the story of this fragment, we are actively looking for ways to fuel our debates and support our agendas. We should also expect that these debates and agendas will bleed into our historical portraits as well.

CHALLENGES

In the first two centuries after Mary Magdalene's death she went from disciple, to obscurity, to a target for misogyny. Her legacy was confused with Mary of Bethany, the sister of Martha and Lazarus. Parallel to this progression, Mary became the ideal and transcendent disciple, and an object of jealousy. From the Middle Ages onward, she became the harbinger of vices. Twelve hundred years after she died, she became inexplicably wealthy. She was royalty, owner of a walled city, but tragically given to sensuality. In short, Mary Magdalene became a prostitute in the imaginations of the Christianized West. She became the exemplary sinner and the model of penitence during the Reformation. In the modern world – sexualized as she was – she became a modern, worldly woman. She was the object of Jesus' desire and temptation. She became the lover of Jesus and then, finally, the wife of Jesus.

At each turn, Mary Magdalene reflected the debates and agendas of those who imagined her. Our latest notion that she was the wife of Jesus must reflect something about us as a culture. Her recent marriage to Jesus is an opportunity for us to become more aware of ourselves. Otherwise we unwittingly project ourselves onto our discoveries.

FURTHER READING

Esther A. de Boer and John Bowden, *The Mary Magdalene Cover-Up: The Sources Behind the Myth* (London: T & T Clark, 2006).

Bart D. Ehrman, *Truth and Fiction in* The Da Vinci Code: *A Historian Reveals What We Really Know about Jesus, Mary Magdalene, and Constantine* (Oxford: Oxford University Press, 2004).

Darren J. N. Middleton, *Scandalizing Jesus?: Kazantzakis's* The Last Temptation of Christ *Fifty Years On* (London: Bloomsbury, 2005).

Jane Schaberg with Melanie Johnson-Debaufre, *Mary Magdalene Understood* (New York: Continuum, 2006).

SMITHING JESUS

"God created man in his own image.
And man, being a gentleman,
returned the favor."

– JEAN-JACQUES ROUSSEAU

Our portraits of Jesus are constantly shifting, adapting, and evolving to suit our agendas and ideals. Groups, both inside and outside the Christian mainstream, have leveraged Jesus against their opponents, or done so to justify their own practices. That said, there is much about Jesus that remains seemingly unchanged. As a figure of our collective imagination, Jesus is most often a celibate, heterosexual man. Portraits that suggest otherwise are jarring and can, at times, reveal something about the dominant values of the Christianized West.

Jamaican-American artist Renée Cox poked at these norms with her photographic homage to Da Vinci's *Last Supper*. Her series of photographs titled *Yo Mama's Last Supper* depicts Jesus as an almost nude black woman. When this series was featured at the Brooklyn Museum of Art in 2001, then mayor Rudolph Giuliani called it "disgusting," "outrageous," and "anti-Catholic."[1]

It is easy to understand the offense taken. In a culture where mixing sexuality and religion is uncomfortable, a nude, womanist portrait of Jesus is bound to scandalize. It should be pointed out, however, that an almost nude (sometimes entirely nude) Jesus on the cross is commonplace and offends very few people – importantly, this Jesus is usually white and male. Cox's Jesus portrait, aside from being a nude, is not erotically suggestive. Her Jesus is rigid, stoic, and looks heavenward. Judging from Giuliani's reaction, a nude, black, womanist portrait of Jesus is more offensive than a nude, white, male portrait.

Pablo Picasso once said that "art is a lie that tells the truth." While some, like Giuliani, express disgust, others see the image of a black Jesus or a woman Jesus as an opportunity to critique our

Crucifixion (*c.* 1541), Michelangelo. This chalk drawing accentuates the musculature of Jesus. Those familiar with his famous Sistine Chapel ceiling will recognize a similar exaggeration of physique. Here Jesus wears only a hint of a loin cloth, allowing the artist to unify the dominant vertical lines of shading. Like most nude or almost nude portraits of Jesus, the starkness of clothing is not suggestive of sexuality – even when Jesus' physique is the key subject.

more familiar portraits. Why is the Scandinavian Jesus of Warner Sallman more acceptable than a Jamaican Jesus? This point has been made so often in recent years that it has almost become banal to criticize Sallman's *Head of Christ*.[2] But we risk repeating the same error when we refuse to allow our assumptions of Jesus' sexuality (or non-sexuality) to be challenged.

Even more critical is the way that common portraits reinforce systems of power. Because Jesus has been so often coopted by the powerful, recent attempts to subvert power have coopted Jesus to

Head of Christ (c. 1940), Warner Sallman. Sallman's Jesus with Scandinavian features has become one of the most recognized portraits in American art. This image was reproduced in several inexpensive prints, greeting cards, and so on to make it almost ubiquitous in evangelical churches across North America.

push back against the image. In what follows, I will discuss two forms of sexual persecution that resulted in new portraits of Jesus – both present Jesus as a sexual being who is dissimilar from the standard celibate heterosexual portrait. The first sexualized Jesus comes from the early Mormons as they developed into a polygamous people. The second Jesus comes from twentieth-century gay America.

JESUS THE PROTO-MORMON POLYGAMIST

When Mormonism was in its infancy, there was very little talk of "plural marriage." The book of Mormon (c. 1820–29) says nothing of the doctrine. Joseph Smith Jr., the founder of the movement, introduced the doctrine in the 1840s after he had been "sealed to" multiple wives. Still, there was a concerted effort to keep Smith's polygamy a secret from the general public. Emerging from an evangelical, American mainstream, the practice of plural marriage alienated the early Mormons from their religious neighbors.[3] Indeed, it was a difficult teaching to adopt for the inner circle of leaders.

Brigham Young was among the original apostles of the Mormons, the second president of the movement, and founder of Salt Lake City, Utah. Before becoming Smith's successor, Young worked beneath Smith in Nauvoo, Illinois. It was in Nauvoo that Smith first introduced the idea of plural marriage. In John G. Turner's biography of Brigham Young he describes Young's early aversion to the idea of polygamy:

> At some point in early 1842, Smith told [Brigham Young] to "go & get another wife." Young recalled that the instruction came in the form of a "command," not a choice. Still, he hesitated. "I felt as if the grave was better for me," he later explained. After discussing the matter with Smith, though,

the apostle quickly moved from apprehension to exhilaration. "I was filled with the Holy Ghost . . . I could jump and hollow [holler], my blood clear as India Rum." Young was "ready to go ahead." Like many others, he followed where his prophet led. No one would marry more women in Nauvoo than Brigham Young.[4]

Before Young's death in 1877, he had been "sealed to" as many as fifty-five women. He wed girls as young as fifteen and women as old as sixty-five. He wed widows, single women, and women who were already married to other men. He even wed two of his mothers-in-law. Moreover, Young became convinced that the doctrine of plural marriage was divinely ordained. Eventually, this sexual ethic was projected onto both God the Father and Jesus. Late in life, Young wrote: "Said [Jesus], when talking to his disciples: 'He that hath seen me hath seen the Father;' and, 'I and my Father are one.' The Scripture says that He, the Lord, came walking in the Temple,

"A Mormon and his wives dancing to the devil's tune" (c.1850). This lithograph illustrates the repulsion evoked by the Mormon practice of plural marriage. Drawn and published by I. M. Van Duesen, a disenchanted Mormonite.

with His train; I do not know who they were, unless His wives and children . . . "[5]

To understand Young's logic here, one must recognize three steps. First, Jesus reflects the image of God. Young makes this point quite forcefully leading up to his two citations of John's Gospel. Moreover, Young believed that the family unit reflected the image of God. Second, God is literally a father. Quoting the biblical prophet Isaiah, Young suggests that God is married many times over with numerous children. This point is made by appealing to the King James Translation: ". . . I saw also the Lord sitting upon a throne, high and lifted up, and his train filled the temple."[6] In the King James Bible "his train" is translated vaguely, allowing Young to suppose that the Lord is followed by his family. Third, Jesus, reflecting divine reality, reflects the truth of plural marriage. Young writes: "The same truth is borne out by the Savior."[7]

Seemingly it took years for Young to come to the belief that Jesus practiced plural marriage. As Young's early distaste for the idea indicates, plural marriage was far afield from popular American notions of normalcy. He became a defender of its legitimacy only after being persuaded by Smith and his encounter with the "Holy Ghost." Taken to the next level, plural marriage was more than legitimate; it reflected God's own practice. Finally, Jesus, as God's son, was probably polygamous. This logic probably relates to Young's famous saying, "The only men who become Gods, even Sons of God, are those who enter into polygamy."[8]

A similar development can be seen in the theology of Orson Pratt, the first public advocate for Mormon plural marriage. Orson Pratt was among the earliest Mormons; he was an apostle, and a missionary. In 1839, Pratt and his wife Sarah Marinda Bates Pratt settled in western Illinois alongside a number of other Mormons. Most of the town was bought by the Mormons and governed by

Joseph Smith. While Orson was in Europe seeking converts, Joseph Smith made repeated advances on Sarah Pratt, against her wishes. According to interviews given by Sarah and another Mormon leader named John C. Bennett, Smith attempted to make her one of his "spiritual wives." After resisting these advances multiple times in secret, Sarah informed her husband who had recently returned from his missionary work.

Orson Pratt confronted Smith and told him to "never offer an insult of the like again."[9] The sordid controversy that followed is too long to recount here, but it resulted in the excommunication of Orson Pratt and John C. Bennett. Shortly thereafter, Orson Pratt's apostasy was forgotten and the Pratt family was officially restored. Sarah Pratt, however, would never regain her good reputation. Joseph Smith accused her of adultery with John C. Bennett, and she spent the next twenty-five years contending with this label.

Orson Pratt defended his wife's honor and never publicly confirmed Smith's accusations.[10] But over the next few years Orson came to support the doctrine of plural marriage and sealed himself to multiple wives without Sarah's consent:[11] "The pressures to conform to the polygamous social order were not subtle. Sarah reluctantly went along with the system for almost a quarter of a century."[12] After giving birth to ten children, after multiple missionary journeys that took the lives of four of these children, after living in poverty for much of her life, and after becoming estranged from her husband, Sarah Pratt finally separated from Orson. She told much of this story in an interview given to the *New York Herald*.[13]

It was within this context that Orson Pratt became the first public advocate for Mormon polygamy. Soon after his initial conflict with Smith, Pratt became convinced of the new divine command for plural marriage. Brigham Young then commanded Orson Pratt to preach and publish publicly in support of plural marriage. It is noteworthy that Young issued this command only after several stories began to circulate concerning Smith's plural marriages.

In an 1853 article titled "Celestial Marriage," Pratt argued that Jesus (like his ancestors) was a polygamist. He appealed to several parabolic or poetic passages from the Bible to argue that Jesus took multiple wives. Pratt quoted John the Baptist who said, "He that hath the bride is the bridegroom, but the friend of the bridegroom, which standeth and heareth him, rejoiceth greatly because of the bridegroom's voice."[14] Pratt also quoted Jesus who said, "Can the children of the bridechamber mourn, as long as the bridegroom is with them? But the days will come, when the bridegroom shall be taken from them . . . "[15] As seen here, both biblical passages refer to Jesus as a "bridegroom." Taken literally, these passages demonstrate that Jesus was married.

In order to demonstrate that Jesus practiced plural marriage, Pratt appealed to the royal wedding of Psalm 45 and argued that the royal figure of that psalm was Jesus. Pratt concluded that "the great Messiah, who was the founder of the Christian religion, was a polygamist, as well as the Patriarch Jacob and the Prophet David, from whom he descended according to the flesh." According to Pratt, Jesus practiced plural marriage to provide an example for future generations. Indeed, "by marrying many honorable wives himself, [Jesus would] show all future generations that he approbated the plurality of Wives under the Christian dispensation, as well as under the dispensations in which His Polygamist ancestors lived."[16]

Much like the early Mormon movement itself, Pratt's stance on polygamy can be divided into three periods. In the 1830s and early 1840s he had no inclination toward the practice – perhaps no thought of it whatsoever. When the practice was introduced by Smith in the 1840s, Pratt was repulsed by it, calling it an "insult" to the honor of his marriage. We can safely say that Pratt's strong belief in monogamous marriage was part and parcel with the sensibilities of nineteenth-century America at large. Sometime in the mid-1840s, however, Pratt became fully convinced that the doctrine of plural marriage was of divine command and required of him. By the early 1850s, Smith's beliefs about marriage and family had been projected onto the life of Jesus.

Consider a similar claim made by Mormon leader Jedediah M. Grant. Like Young and Pratt, Grant portrayed Jesus as a polygamist. Grant took this a step further by supporting it with a veneer of historical research. He wrote:

> What does old Celsus say, who was a physician in the first century, whose medical works are esteemed very highly at the present time. His works on theology were burned with fire by the Catholics, they were so shocked at what they called their impiety. Celsus was a heathen philosopher; and what does he say upon the subject of Christ and his Apostles, and their belief? He says "The grand reason why the Gentiles and philosophers of his school persecuted Jesus Christ, was, because he had so many wives; there were Elizabeth, and Mary, and a host of others that followed him." After Jesus went from the stage of action, the apostles followed the example of their master.[17]

Grant concluded that Jesus' crucifixion "was evidently based upon polygamy, according to the testimony of the philosophers who rose in that age. A belief in the doctrine of a plurality of wives caused the persecution of Jesus and his followers. We might almost think they were 'Mormons.'"[18] This last comment is telling and will be revisited below. But first, three observations are warranted.

First, Grant is misinformed. The first-century medical philosopher named "Celsus" to which he refers never makes any statements about Jesus. In fact, the works of Aulus Cornelius Celsus (born *c.* 25 B.C.E.) do not include any theological subjects at all. It is highly likely that Grant has the wrong Celsus. The "heathen philosopher" who is known for his statements about Jesus and Christianity lived approximately one hundred years later. Grant probably has the second-century Celsus in mind.

Second, neither the first-century Celsus nor the second-century Celsus claim that Jesus had "so many wives." At first glance this quotation seems to be wholesale fabrication. Placed between direct quotation marks, as seen above, Grant seems to have invented this quotation to support the new Mormon agenda. But there is another option, one that paints Grant in a less duplicitous light. A third-century Christian named Origen wrote against a different

---

CELSUS

Celsus was a second-century Greek philosopher who is best known today for his sustained attack on Christianity. His work is known to us only through the work of Christian apologist Origen. Origen's "Against Celsus" (written in the third century) quotes Celsus extensively. Celsus' counter-arguments against Christian doctrine include the claim that Jesus was fathered by a Roman man named "Panthera." He assumes that Jesus did perform amazing feats, but accuses Jesus of having learned "magic" during his time in Egypt. In the world of Jesus and Celsus, the accusation of magical practice was always considered an insult. Origen's quotations of Celsus are valuable as they provide an outsider's perspective on early Christianity.

philosopher named Celsus. In a work titled *Against Celsus*, Origen writes:

> . . . such was the charm of Jesus' words, that not only were men willing to follow him to the wilderness, but women also, forgetting the weakness of their sex and a regard for outward propriety in thus following their Teacher into desert places.[19]

This statement by Origen is meant to explain "what stirred up the envy of the Jews against Jesus, and aroused them to conspire against him." Simply put, according to Origen, Jesus was persecuted and killed because of his popularity and large following. As a side note, this following included many women who had forgotten their station and acted without propriety.

Grant might have heard another Mormon preacher refer to "Celsus" on this point and misquoted him. I think it is highly likely that Grant never read this text for himself. This solution explains Grant's confusion about the two philosophers. While I will not rule out duplicity on Grant's part, the better solution is that Grant came by this error honestly. In either case, the words attributed to Celsus here were authored in the nineteenth century, not the first century. Grant's quotation from "Celsus" is still used to support a polygamous portrait of Jesus in some corners of Mormonism.

The third observation is that Grant's portrait of Jesus reflects the chief concerns of the mid-1850s for Mormon leadership: the persecution of Joseph Smith and his followers and accusations of polygamy.[20] Much like the interpretations of Young and Pratt, Jedediah Grant paints Jesus as a polygamist. The desire to find an authoritative justification for their misunderstood religious practice was so great that Grant (perhaps unwittingly) manufactured historical evidence. In doing so, he was convinced that polygamy was the very cause of Jesus' martyrdom. "We might almost think they were 'Mormons,'" Grant concludes.

The early Mormons patterned their movement after early Christianity. They received visions, appended "new" testaments to sacred canons, appointed twelve "Apostles," and so on. But conversely, the early Mormons patterned early Christianity after themselves. Jesus became a prototypical Mormon. These early Mormon theologians projected Joseph Smith's sexuality onto Jesus.

JESUS, GAY MAN OF MYSTERY

In a 2010 interview with *Parade* magazine, singer and songwriter Elton John was quoted as saying, "I think Jesus was a compassionate, super-intelligent gay man who understood human problems." John, in addition to being a Rock and Roll Hall of Fame inductee, is a philanthropist and a long-time advocate for the gay, lesbian, bisexual, transgendered community. To this end, he has often spoken publicly of his life as a gay man, husband, and father. Speaking of Jesus, John said, "On the cross, he forgave the people who crucified him. Jesus wanted us to be loving and forgiving. I don't know what makes people so cruel."[21]

In response to John's interview, ABC News sought a response from Catholic League president, Bill Donohue. Donohue chided John, saying that "to call Jesus a homosexual is to label Him a sexual deviant." A more considered response came from Rev. Sharon Ferguson. I will include her comments in a larger excerpt of the ABC News article to illustrate the marketing motives at work in this controversy. Ferguson demurs in response to John's claim:

> "I don't think that comments like this are particularly helpful," Reverend Sharon Ferguson from the Lesbian and Gay Christian Movement told ABC News.

"He challenged our understanding of loving one another in his relationship with his disciples and friends, so we should be taking on board the total inclusivity of Christ when it comes to the notion of sexual identity and orientation but that does not mean that we should make any assumptions about Christ's sexual activity or lack of it."

Whatever the fallout, it puts the Rocket Man firmly in the eye of a storm of controversy, once again. The magazine is out on newsstands Saturday.[22]

Notice that there are at least four agendas at work in this story. Elton John's agenda seems to include advocacy for a group that has historically been persecuted, and especially so in the Christianized West. Bill Donohue's agenda seems to include a defense of a more traditional view of sexual normalcy. Sharon Ferguson seems to value reconciliation between an often exclusive Church and a historically persecuted group. Finally, both *Parade* magazine and ABC News seem to be publicizing this controversy to sell a product. The commonality among all four is that the name "Jesus" is wielded to advance an agenda. For better or worse, Jesus' name is an ideological force. This has been true in Christendom for two millennia and is no less true in the world of pop culture, LGBT advocacy,[23] and capitalist enterprise.

This, of course, is just one narrow window into a much larger debate about sexuality and gender in the Christianized West. It is quite common for Jesus' name to be dropped into such conversations. In my own experience, I most often hear advocates for gay equality remind us what Jesus did *not* say. For example, former U.S. president Jimmy Carter said, "Homosexuality was well known in the ancient world, well before Christ was born and Jesus never said a word about homosexuality."[24] But claims about Jesus such as that made by Elton John are becoming more common.[25] Not coincidentally, the possibility that Jesus was homosexual is a relatively new talking point among historians.[26]

Jimmy Carter is quite right: various sexual lifestyles were known in the ancient world. While the modern concept of "gay" is relatively new, homoeroticism is nothing new. But the role that this played in early Christianity is a topic that was untouched by scholars before the twentieth century. Elton John's gay Jesus is an extension of a controversy that began in 1960.

The scholar who brought the notion of a gay Jesus to the international stage was a mercurial figure named Morton Smith (1915–91). Smith was a seminary-trained priest who, very early in his career, chose a life in academia. Like most clergy who choose this path, Smith maintained his official affiliation with the Church. At least, he did so for most of his career. But his students and colleagues knew that there was much more to Morton Smith. His student Albert Baumgarten wrote that early in Smith's career he "left the church, characterizing the position he came to adopt as atheism."[27]

Morton Smith's deep (often hostile) misgivings toward traditional Christianity bled through and into his publications, even in his early career. He received two doctorates, one from Hebrew University in Jerusalem and the other from Harvard Divinity School. A close colleague wrote that Smith's doctoral dissertation "was the first of many studies calculated to enrage the Establishment, Jewish or Christian, but far too intelligent and erudite to be dismissed as simply annoying."[28] Smith's early career as a highly intelligent provocateur lit a fuse that would launch him to global recognition in 1973.

According to Smith, he discovered an ancient letter written by Clement of Alexandria (c. 150–c. 215), recopied in the eighteenth century into the back pages of another book, and preserved in a Greek Orthodox monastery south of Jerusalem. What would make this particular letter unique was that it included a previously unknown story about Jesus from a purportedly longer version of Mark's Gospel. The story describes Jesus raising a wealthy young man from the dead and then spending the night with him.

Smith claimed to have discovered this document in 1958 and announced the find in 1960. He didn't publish his books on the subject until 1973. He called his discovery *The Secret Gospel According to Mark*. Most scholars today call the text *Secret Mark*.

This "gospel" comes to us as an excerpt quoted in an ancient letter to a disciple named "Theodore." In this letter, Clement (the supposed author) instructs Theodore against the demonically inspired teaching of a heretic named Carpocrates. According to the letter, Carpocrates obtained an authentic gospel. Indeed, Clement says that this mystical gospel conveyed "spotless" and "holy words". What made the teachings of Carpocrates heretical was thus not the text of *Secret Mark*, but the misinterpretation of this text. The text of *Secret Mark* has been "mixed with shameless lies" (I.10).

Clement goes on to explain that the text of the "mystical" gospel was indeed written by Mark – the same author who wrote the biblical Gospel by the same name. But, curiously, Clement instructs Theodore to lie about its authorship in public so as to guard the truth. Clement justifies this deceit by quoting the Hebrew proverb: "Answer the fool from his folly" (Prov. 26:5). The reader, it seems, is told that foolish people do not deserve the truth. Clement cites Ecclesiastes 2:14: "let the fool walk in darkness." The author instructs the reader to lie even if under oath about the true authorship of the letter.

Whoever authored this letter seems to think that there is virtue in falsehood about the origins of *Secret Mark*.

The supposed Clement then reveals what this mystical gospel really says. He quotes the "very words" of this gospel to answer Theodore's questions (I.20–21). Clement begins his direct quotation of *Secret Mark*. In this setting, Jesus raises a young man from the dead and then stays the night with him:

"And gazing at him, the young man loved him and began to plead with him that he might be with him. . . . they went into the young man's house." After this, Jesus summons the young man who is "wearing a linen cloth over his naked body." He "stayed with him that night, for Jesus taught him the mystery of the kingdom of God" (II.2–10). Clement explains that: "After this, it adds, 'James and John went to him,' and all that section, but 'naked man with naked man' and the other things about which you wrote, are not found." To modern ears, the phrase "spent the night with" and the rumor of "naked man with naked man" is immediately suggestive.

When Smith announced this discovery in 1960, it raised immediate suspicion among biblical scholars, not least because it seemingly supported "not only Smith's love of controversy but also his favorite target."[29] For such a provocative discovery to come from a known provocateur seemed far too convenient. To fuel this suspicion, the original document mysteriously disappeared and was unable to undergo the full battery of tests that are standard for such discoveries.[30] Indeed, only a handful of scholars laid eyes on the document before it was "misplaced" (hidden? destroyed?) by its handlers at the monastery. But this did not stop widespread media coverage about the text, its implications, and Smith's motives. Bruce Chilton, a colleague of Smith, writes:

> Press coverage proved wide and instantaneous, because "Secret Mark" climaxes with an evocative image: A young man who wore only "a linen cloth over his naked body" spends the night with Jesus, who "taught him the mystery of the kingdom of God." That proved too good a lure to pass up: What reader of the Gospels could fail to wonder whether Jesus engaged in the sexually charged initiation that "Secret Mark" describes?

Smith himself, a homosexual at a time when homophobia ran high, had little doubt.[31]

Chilton represents many scholars in thinking that Morton Smith authored *Secret Mark* to provide a homosexual portrait of Jesus. Moreover, as Chilton rightly points out, the timing of Smith's "discovery" is as telling as anything else. While a great deal could be said about the humiliation, incarceration, beating, electroconvulsive experimentation, and murder of homosexuals during this period, for the present we can confirm that homophobia ran high indeed.[32] The vast majority of Church officials were either silent or firmly set against gay advocacy. It should also be pointed out that gay advocacy was barely conceived during this period of American history. The movement was well under way, however, when Smith published his two books on *Secret Mark* in 1973.[33]

Morton Smith cared deeply about this issue as early as 1949 when he wrote of the deep rift between traditional Christianity and homosexual well-being. He wrote (hypothetically) of a young man – a new convert – who seeks counseling from a Christian counselor. Smith explained that this young man "doesn't see that if two adult males enjoy each other sexually, any harm is done to anybody." Smith goes on: "He doesn't seem to be unstable, keeps his job, gets on well in society, has lots of normal friends, and seems generally happy. And, after all, homosexuality has been a characteristic of some of the greatest men – Plato and Shakespeare, etc."

How must the Christian counselor instruct this young man? Smith wrote:

> He must be told that homosexuality is a sin far more serious than fornication, and that unwillingness or inability to repent of it automatically debars the sinner from the sacraments. Whether or not psychological or social arguments against

homosexuality are used, it must be made clear that the sin is not
a matter for dispute nor for private judgment, but is established
by the Christian tradition which individuals can only accept or
reject. Finally, for the good of the congregation no less than
for his own good, he must sooner or later be made to choose
between his new attachment to the Church and his previous
sexual adjustment, even though there be great probability that
he will find no other adjustment so satisfactory.[34]

Smith concluded that it was almost impossible for a homosexual
to be "happy" as a member of the body of Christ.[35] He wrote this
as a member of the clergy, long before his own sexual orientation
was widely discussed among his colleagues. For the present, it is
less important that Smith be labeled "gay" or "bisexual" and more
relevant that we note his sincere concern for this topic. According
to Smith, the homosexual male must choose happiness outside of
the bounds of Christian communion or (most likely) unhappiness
within it.

At this point, allow me to state the obvious: it is incredible to
believe that a scholar who had previously published on the topic of
homosexuality, in a context wherein the topic was so extremely rare
in public discourse, just happened to find an ancient document so
relevant for gay advocacy. Just as the Gay P.R.I.D.E. movement was
throwing off the shackles of legal oppression in the United States,
Morton Smith was writing these words: "Freedom from [Jewish
religious] law may have resulted in a completion of the spiritual
union by physical union."[36]

Let me underscore that I'm not suggesting that because Smith was
concerned for homosexual well-being that he must have invented
this document. The key here is evidence of a discontentment
strong enough to take action. Those closest to Smith observed
this very tendency in his character. Smith "enjoyed provoking the

conventionally faithful, proposing reconstructions of the past that opposed the narrative promoted by Jewish and Christian orthodoxies."[37]

A great deal has been written on Morton Smith and *Secret Mark*. The story is just too bizarre not to attract attention. Those who are convinced that Smith's gospel was a hoax argue that the document contains clues left by the author to reveal his identity. They further argue that the document contains the very twentieth-century euphemism "stayed the night with", and that in the ancient world this euphemism would not have indicated coitus.

Perhaps most telling is that Smith's story seems to parody an evangelical novel written in 1940 called *The Mystery of Mar Saba*.[38] It is the story of a discovery of an ancient document that embarrasses traditional Christianity. The book was so popular in the 1940s that it

"Photograph of Mar Saba" (*c.* 1895). Mar Saba is a Greek Orthodox monastery. It is one of the oldest inhabited monasteries in the world.

warranted at least nine printings. Smith visited Mar Saba for the first time one year after the novel was published, the very place where he would eventually "discover" his own mysterious document. In many publications, Smith seems to borrow phrases directly from this novel. After detailing parallels of location, content, descriptions of discovery, and vocabulary, New Testament scholar Francis Watson concludes: "The parallels are such that the question of dependence is unavoidable . . . There is no alternative but to conclude that Smith is dependent on the novel, and that he himself is the author of the fragments of the Secret Gospel of Mark together with the pseudo-Clementine letter in which they are embedded."[39]

Finally, it should be noted that one of the heroes of the novel is named "Lord Moreton," a name phonetically identical to "Morton." The most likely solution is that Morton Smith was inspired and repulsed by this evangelical novel while writing his dissertation in Jerusalem, and decided to expose evangelical foolishness with a hoax of his own. Most biblical scholars now think that the document was probably authored by Smith himself. But there is a vocal minority that is convinced of its authenticity. Many argue that Smith could not have authored this document himself. While handwriting experts have offered mixed conclusions, the document seems to be remarkably similar to the style of Clement of Alexandria. Those who are convinced that Smith forged the document must acknowledge the sheer brilliance it would take to fool so many people, including experts.

Some have argued that Smith appeared to take his research on *Secret Mark* quite seriously. Others think he delighted in the froth that he had stirred up, reserving the right to be indignant when overly conservative agendas were laid bare. For my part, I think that he was a brilliant trickster, and wanted his hoax to live on long past his death. Truly, it is hard not to admire how utterly clever the man was. Smith's gospel contributed to the gay advocacy movement at just the right time, and continues to voice the concerns that he first explored in his essay on gay psychology and Christian unhappiness.[40] Whether a hoax or not, its entry into the American consciousness was brilliantly timed. Carlson observes that *Secret Mark*:

> was written during the 1950's, during an especially oppressive moment in American history when mainline ministers were urging the police to crack down on gay men gathered in public parks. What could be more upsetting to the Establishment in this historical moment than the intimation, revealed in an ancient text by the author of the oldest gospel, that they are crucifying Jesus Christ all over again?[41]

Smith's retelling of Christian beginnings certainly reflects the spirit of his time. One might say that Smith's gay Jesus remained a secret in the 1950s, came out of the closet in the 1960s, and became a public advocate in the 1970s. Along this timeline, Jesus was just one step ahead of Elton John.

CHALLENGES

In the case of Mormon visionary Joseph Smith, we saw that his own investment toward normalizing polygamy came before his divine instructions on the topic. We saw that his apostles had to warm to this new vision of sexual normalcy. Their arguments for a polygamous Jesus then served to legitimize themselves in the face of persecution. Finally, whether by intention or misunderstanding, they manufactured an ancient document by "Celsus" to support their cause. In the case of Morton Smith, we saw that his investment in the topic of gay angst within the Church came before his discovery of *Secret Mark*. In both cases, the persecution of a sexually "deviant" community created the context for the reception of previously unknown portraits of Jesus.

For most of us, spotting the agendas and ideologies at work in others seems easy. Many people have probably never considered the notion that Jesus had multiple wives or that he was gay, and so they will be cautious about these sexualized portraits from the beginning. But recognizing our own agendas and ideological projections onto Jesus is more difficult. If we are to be honest and avoid the arrogance of creating Jesus in our own image, a healthy suspicion of ourselves is warranted. The challenge for us, therefore, is to examine the agendas and ideologies that we unwittingly project onto Jesus. This is not to say that all of our projections are wrong, or that they can be avoided entirely. It simply questions the arrogance of assuming that our agendas are more benign than that of Joseph Smith or Morton Smith.

FURTHER READING

Tony Burke (ed.), *Ancient Gospel or Modern Forgery? The Secret Gospel of Mark in Debate: Proceedings from the 2011 York University Christian Apocrypha Symposium* (Eugene: Wipf & Stock, 2013).

Douglas J. Davies, *An Introduction to Mormonism* (Cambridge: Cambridge University Press, 2003).

Dale B. Martin, *Sex and the Single Savior: Gender and Sexuality in Biblical Interpretation* (Louisville: Westminster John Knox Press, 2006).

John G. Turner, *Brigham Young: Pioneer, Prophet* (Cambridge, MA: Belknap Press of Harvard University, 2012).

FROM PERSIA, WITH LOVE

Happy love has no history. Romance only comes into existence where love is fatal, frowned upon and doomed by life itself.

– DENIS DE ROUGEMENT

The first line of Dave Matthew's "Christmas Song" refers to Jesus' parents: "She was his girl; he was her boyfriend." When Jesus meets "another Mary" his heart is full of "love, love, love." I discussed this song more fully in chapter 4, where I also discussed the early frames of Cecil B. DeMille's *King of Kings,* in which Mary of Magdala was called a "courtesan." In Veronica Patterson's "love poem" (also discussed in chapter 4) she hints at a sexual tension between Jesus and Mary. In these portraits and in many others we see the influence of romantic or "courtly love."

This should come as no surprise; romance is one of our most celebrated themes in the Christianized West. A love story can be a potent and effective vehicle to drive a narrative. When modern storytellers want to humanize a character, adding a "love interest" is quite common. Given that the iconic Jesus has always been just above humanization, it was only a matter of time before modern storytellers attempted to humanize him: adding romance to his story is perhaps part and parcel of our attempt to do this.

It is hard to blame these popular storytellers. Romance and the pursuit of love is so much a part of our cultural psyche that we can hardly help but explore Jesus' emotions. Furthermore, we should expect that Jesus experienced a full range of human emotions. Of course, a "full range" of emotions varies from person to person, and while there are probably several analogies to be drawn between Jesus' culture and ours, caution is warranted. One major difference between the two cultures is the importance of emotional motivation for marriage. While modern, Western marriage is built on the freedom to choose a mate on the basis of romantic courtship and mutual affection, this was not the world in which Jesus lived. Any exploration of the wife of Jesus must account for these differences. In Jesus' culture, there were no "boyfriends," as Dave Matthews imagines; the word "romance" had not been coined, and "courtly love" – what we moderns just think of as "love" – was not a primary motivation for marriage.

IMPASSABLE BARRIERS

In human history, romance is a relatively new motivation for marriage. I won't be able to provide a detailed history of romantic love in this book, but it might be helpful to point to a few historical developments that stand between us and the ancient culture of Jesus.

Concerning "chemistry," one might point as far back as four million years when "the first cascades of neurochemicals flowing from the brain produced goofy grins and sweaty palms as men and women gazed deeply into each other's eyes."[1] Or one might imagine that the modern, Western notion of romantic love has been deeply influenced by commercial culture. Perhaps the words of fictional *Mad Men* ad executive, Don Draper, ring true: "What you call love was invented by guys like me to sell nylons."[2] Erotic pursuits are as old as the hills and as new as Madison Avenue. But when did erotic attraction become romantic love? And when did romantic love become the primary motive to marry?

Those familiar with the Hebrew Bible will remember the intense emotion and physical intimacy described in the Song of Songs. It is, however, important to remember that this poem describes the playful exploits of the wealthy and not the common "courtship" of regular people. Moreover, it is not clear that the partners in the Song of Songs are consummating their marriage.[3] This helps to illustrate an important point: eroticism is an important part of the human experience, but it has *not* always been a primary reason to marry.

While the developments of "romantic love" vary from culture to culture, it would be difficult to understate the global impact of medieval Persian poetry. From eighth-century Baghdad (perhaps earlier[4]) to the height of Moorish Spain, love poetry thrived in the Arab world. While many poems focused on the mere physicality of sexual encounter, some poems (usually associated with rural, Bedouin verse) voiced an affection that transcended physicality. The distinction between rural and urban love poetry should not be drawn too neatly, but it does convey a long-held stereotype of Bedouin innocence. Interesting for this chapter is a conversation written by a thirteenth-century scholar named Ibn al-Qayyim. This scholar claims to recount a conversation between an eighth-century urbanite and his rural, Bedouin aunt:

> I [al-Asmāṣ'i] said to a Bedouin woman: "What do you consider love to be among you?"
> "Hugging, embracing, winks, and conversation," she replied.
> The she asked: "How is it among you, city-dweller?"
> "He sits amidst her four limbs (shu 'abihā[5]) and presses her to the limit," I answered.
> "Nephew," she cried, "this is no lover ('ashiq), but a man after a child!"[6]

This conversation supports the general stereotype of relative innocence among rural people and/or commoners. It is also important to recognize a difference between the views of urban males and others. The candid reply of the aunt in this exchange would have seemed novel to the wealthy men of Baghdad in the eighth century, but this notion of mutual affection (rather than mere physicality) would soon become influential among the elite. Bedouin notions of love driven by the vehicles of rural poets were eventually popularized and made famous across the Arab world.

One of these poems (perhaps inspired by Bedouin themes) is titled "Layla and Majnun." This poem tells a story of unrequited love.[7] Attributed to a seventh-century poet named Qays ibn al-Mulawwah, the poor shepherd poet pursues a childhood friend named Layla. When her father refuses the match and marries Layla to another man, the poet is driven mad and retreats to the wilderness. This is how he receives the name "Majnun," which means "possessed" or "madman." Both Majnun and Layla die separated, in grief. As the legend goes, the corpse of the poet is found beside the tomb of a nameless woman whereupon he has scratched his verse.

Famously, the story of Layla and Majnun inspired the blues/rock hit "Layla" by Derek and the Dominos. But, until its incarnation on the 1970s music scene, the tragic legend of Layla and Majnun reached an apex of popularity in the twelfth century. Unlike many sexually explicit poems, this poem demonstrates a kind of love that is never consummated. It is therefore something of a departure from simple eroticism.

We might also point to a collection of poems from the tenth century by a poet named al-Sarraj. This popular collection is titled *Masari al-Ushshaq*, which translates into "Battle of Lovers" or "Death of Lovers." These poets were "falling" in love centuries before Eric Clapton crooned "I'm falling on my knees, Layla!" But more importantly for this chapter is the entry point of this Persian art form into Western consciousness.

Layla and Majnun (*c.* 18th century). This Keshan carpet is based on the story made famous by the twelfth-century poet Nizami Ganjavi. The rag-clad "madman" on the left is surrounded by wild beasts and foliage, suggesting his eventual retreat from civilized society.

The period when poems such as "Layla and Majnun" and collections such as *Masari al-Ushshaq* were widely known in the Arab world corresponded with the height of Moorish Spain. It is highly probable that this is when romantic courtship emerged in the Western world. Echoing their European Arab neighbors, a wandering band of French poets called the "troubadours" of Occitania became popular in the twelfth and thirteenth centuries. It is possible that the name "troubadour" derives from the Arabic word "taraba," which means "to sing."

These French poets and musicians turned the affection of elite "ladies" into a noble pursuit. Key themes in their music included "humiliation to the lady, love as a means of spiritual improvement, the exclusive focus on married women of superior rank." The troubadours, "had a single term for the ensemble of emotions and behavior they sang about: they called it *fin' amors*, literally 'fine love.'"[8] It is now common to call this "courtly love."

Many of these songs portray lovesick men falling over themselves attempting to woo an objectified – almost deified – woman. In these portraits, the elite "lady" has the power to accept or reject the humiliated suitor, and she often rejects him. Consider this give-and-take between lover and lady:

> Gui d'Ussel, I'll ask you this: when a lady
> Freely loves a man, should she do
> As much for him as he for her,
> According to the rules of courtly love?

> Lady Maria, my reply is this:
> That the lady ought to do exactly
> For her lover as he does for her,
> Without regard to rank.

> Gui, the lover humbly ought to ask
> For everything his heart desires,
> And the lady should comply,
> And she should honor him the way
> She would a friend, but never as a lord.

> Lady, here the people say
> That when a lady wants to love
> She owes her lover equal honor,
> Since they're equally in love.

> Gui, when suitors seek a lady's grace
> They get down on their knees, and say:

Grant that I may freely serve you, Lady,
As your man, and she receives him.

Thus to me it's nothing short of treason
If a man says he's her equal and her servant.[9]

The troubadours do not represent, as some have thought, the monumental shift toward feminism, but their influence marks a decided shift toward courtship as a primary societal value.[10] Propriety and honor were at stake for the man in the winning of a "lady's" affection. Here we see the ideal of elite society stated in terms of reciprocal affection rather than an exchange of property or a fortification of political power. It would take centuries for this ideal to become a common reality, but we see the seeds germinating.

We might say that twelfth-century Europe was not capable of conceiving of equality as we imagine it. It is noteworthy, however, that the conversation of "equal honor" is being openly discussed. Further to this point, we would do well to remember that some of the earliest troubadours were women poets. Scholar of French literature Marilyn Yalom writes:

> Although it is difficult to know how much these songs and stories related to actual practice, it is safe to say that they did affect the way people began to think about love. The invention of romantic love represents what we today call a paradigm shift, one that offered a radically new set of relations between the sexes and one that has had surprisingly long-lasting consequences.[11]

Medievalist C. S. Lewis wrote:

> The troubadours effected a change which has left no corner of our ethics, our imagination, or our daily life untouched, and they erected impassable barriers between us and the classical past and the oriental present.[12]

In fact, it has become commonplace to say that the troubadours *invented* romantic love as we know it. While this is perhaps a Eurocentric overstatement, the point is well taken. Truly, "no corner of our ethic, imagination, or our daily life" is untouched by our desire (need?) for romantic affection.

In the fourteenth century, from the vernacular of Old French, the word "romanz" emerges. The word that once meant "verse narrative" evolved into our concept of "romance" and all that it now implies. This is not to say that erotic love or love poetry did not exist before this period. Of course, the term "erotic" reminds us of the Greek god "Eros" who embodied sexuality and power as early as 700 B.C.E. There can be no doubt that countless commoners across the ancient world felt a deep affection for their partners. But *courtship* (romance as primary motive for marriage) seems to be a medieval development. It should also be noted that erotic attraction had been a factor in choosing a mate long before the medieval period. It is the *centrality* of courtly love that is relatively recent.

The modern, Western concept of marriage is a case in point. Simply put, *we marry for love*. To marry for money, or power, or almost anything else is almost taboo. A "loveless marriage" is commonly seen as grounds for divorce. Undoubtedly it took centuries for the impact of the Persian and French poets to become the common basis for marriage, but the Western world is now driven by romance; it has become fundamental to our psychology and moral fiber. Because of this, it is almost impossible for us to imagine a world where romantic love wasn't the basis for marriage.

C.S. Lewis claims that the explosion of courtly love ideology created "impassable barriers" between the modern, Western mind and the rest of human history and culture. Our preoccupation with romance motivates us, indeed defines us, in profound ways. This perspective on the world stands between us and a clear view of Jesus' culture. It is also important to underscore a point I've made above: eroticism among the social elites (for example, the biblical eroticism of Song of Songs) probably doesn't represent the experiences of common folk. Being of an artisan and farming class, Jesus' life in first-century Galilee would have been dissimilar in a number of ways from those of the social elites such as Antony and Cleopatra. So not only are there cultural barriers between Jesus' culture and ours, there were barriers between the ruling classes and the peasant classes during Jesus' time.

In short, the motivations for and the functions of marriage in Jesus' culture are simply going to seem remote to us. Our inability to imagine a world where courtship is not the basis for marriage is going to be a barrier that hinders our understanding of Jesus' culture.

When we Westerners think of marriage, we think of a relationship built upon mutual affection, desire, and respect. Social and financial stability, extended family considerations, and progeny are often seen as important, but secondary. But in Jesus' culture these priorities were reversed. Social and financial stability, extended family considerations, and progeny were primary. Mutual affection, desire, and respect were often seen as important, but secondary. If we are to take seriously the possibility that Jesus might have been married, we must anticipate motives for marriage that will seem quite alien to us.

GOOD FOR THE CLAN

Another conceptual barrier that stands between our culture and that of Jesus is the difference between individualism and collectivism. An appreciation of these fundamental differences might have a dramatic effect on how we feel about a married Jesus. After all, what if Jesus was arranged to be married when he was still young? In many collectivist cultures, this is not uncommon.

One might think of individualism as a typically Western default position. In general, the countries of Western Europe and those colonized by the British have tended to privilege the rights and well-being of the individual. These cultures also tend to emphasize personal achievement, even at the expense of family or group identities. It is often argued that individualist cultures nurture a greater sense of competition. Collectivist cultures, on the other hand, emphasize family identity and group ideals, often at the expense of individual needs, desires, and achievements.[13] Jesus' culture was closer to what we would call collectivism as compared to modern Western individualism.

An example of collectivism comes from a biblical book called Ezra that was written a few hundred years before the time of Jesus. Ezra tells the story of Israel's displacement and slavery in Babylon and their eventual return. Ezra recounts how Cyrus the Great, King of Persia, helped Ezra's people return to Jerusalem after almost two generations of exile. The Persian king is remembered so fondly for this act that he is called the Lord's "messiah" by the prophet Isaiah.

For the Jews returning from Babylon, this was a chance to rebuild their culture from the ashes of Jerusalem. Ezra the priest was tasked with rebuilding a religion, culture, and ethnicity from the ground up. Ezra, chiefly concerned with the survival of Israel, was not a live-and-let-live sort of fellow. The freedom offered by Cyrus was not nearly enough to restore Israel. According to this story, Israel required a collective identity based on firm cultural boundaries, or it would not survive.

Ezra returns to Jerusalem to find that a group of Jews (who had been living in Judea during the exile) had married ethnic/religious foreigners. When he learns of this, Ezra tears out his beard, rips his clothing, and laments in prayer. Ezra, echoing a command from Deuteronomy, instructs: "Do not give your daughters to their sons, neither take their daughters for your sons."[14] He believed that Jewish–gentile intermarriage would result in collective sin. If Israel didn't repent of this sin collectively, they would be guilty of national disobedience. The majority of the leaders of Judea agree, saying: "We have broken faith with our God and have married foreign women from the peoples of the land, but even now there is hope for Israel in spite of this. So now let us make a covenant with our God to send away all these wives and their children."[15] This story of collective repentance continues:

> Then Ezra the priest stood up and said to them, "You have trespassed and married foreign women, and so increased the guilt of Israel. Now make confession to the Lord the God of your ancestors, and do his will; separate yourselves from the peoples of the land and from the foreign wives." Then all the assembly answered with a loud voice, "It is so; we must do as you have said ... Let our officials represent the whole assembly, and let all in our towns who have taken foreign wives come at appointed times, and with them the elders and judges of every town, until the fierce wrath of our God on this account is averted from us." Only Jonathan son of Asahel and Jahzeiah son of Tikvah opposed this, and Meshullam and Shabbethai the Levites supported them.[16]

This tragic and troubling story concludes: "All these had married foreign women, and they sent them away with their children."[17] I highlight this story for three reasons. First, it illustrates a collectively felt guilt and a collective attempt to restore a social ideal. Second, it illustrates how the identity of the clan can sometimes trump the desires and needs of individuals and individual family units – sometimes with harrowing severity. Third, it speaks directly to marriage expectations. Each of these deserves greater explanation.

In Robert Frost's famous poem, 'Mending Wall,' a cordial neighbor repeats the phrase "good fences make good neighbors."

In this poem, Frost laments the individualism of his culture. From his neighbor's perspective, well-maintained property lines are good. But Frost questions their ultimate virtue. He wonders what he is "walling in" or "walling out" when he builds a fence. He wants to ask "to whom I was like to give offense."[18]

Ezra's first audiences would have had no concept of the kind of alienation voiced by Frost's poem. In the cultures of Ezra and of Jesus, offenses were committed as a group and solved as a group. In cultures of collectivism, your sins are the sins of the entire group, and the collective sins of the group belong to you. Sacred traditions (especially) including marriage norms and taboos served to keep cultural fences intact.

As a child of Western individualism, I am always going to be troubled by Ezra's view of intermarriage. Dividing fathers from their wives and children to rebuild ethnic and religious barriers is going to seem repugnant to me. When I read this, I see racism and dehumanization. But I must admit that my cultural upbringing forces me to focus on the plight of the individuals in this story. I think that I will never know how to read this story from a collectivist perspective. But my cultural perspective should have no claim of superiority over and against others.[19]

This is a story about rebuilding the "necessary walls" around Israel to maintain a culture that is on the brink of extinction. What Ezra knows – in a way that I never will – is that very few borders are more important than marriage norms and taboos. I know that this is the point of the story, but it doesn't make it any less troubling for me. Because of my cultural inclinations, I would much rather have Frost's problem.

Ezra's story of a collective divorce is an extreme example. We should not think that this episode is indicative of common practice among collectivist cultures or Judaism specifically. Historically speaking, we can be relatively certain that this story does not represent a widespread practice. Even in this story, we see that a few individual leaders oppose the will of the clan.[20] Ultimately the ideal communicated in this story shows a unified decision to rebuild a cultural institution.

Sometimes it takes extreme examples to illustrate which ideals a group will defend most fiercely. The Hebrew Bible repeatedly commands care for destitute widows and orphans. Several texts command care for foreigners as well. In this case, however, we see a rare example where the boundaries of group identity are seen to be at odds with the desires and needs of individuals. In this particular example of collectivism, the ideals of group identity are primary – even at the painful expense of individuals.

The third reason I appeal to this story is to illustrate how the ideals of marriage and family reinforce a group's collective identity. Marriage ideals and practices are integral to a culture's sense of stability. Simply put, if you removed all marriage norms and taboos from ancient Israel, you would no longer have a group that resembled ancient Israel. Even reaching back to its earliest network of farming families, marriage ideals were tied to land, food, religious expression, and countless other identity markers. Scholar of ancient Israel, Carol Meyers, writes:

> Just as the family was inextricably connected with its landholdings, so too were individual family members economically and psychologically embedded in the domestic group. As is widely recognized by anyone looking at premodern societies, the concept of the individual and individual identity as we know it today did not yet exist in the biblical world . . . The profound interdependence of family members in self-sufficient agrarian families thus created an atmosphere of corporate family identity, in which one could

conceive not of personal goals and ventures but only of familial ones.[21]

We might allow a few emerging aspects of individuality during the time of Ezra, and perhaps even more during the time of Jesus due to the widespread impact of Greek and Roman ideals.[22] But Ezra provides us with an example of the widespread desire to return to the ideals and practices of previous times. Not all Jews would have agreed with Ezra's vision of reform, but many did.

Of course, illustrations of collectivism can only be taken so far. No doubt there were varying expressions of group identity during Jesus' time. But here is what we can say without qualification: marriage would have been a decision made collectively and for the good of the clan. Even if a patriarchal figure was the guiding force behind the decision, he would not have been an independent agent. There would have been social consequences for moving outside of the bounds of marriage norms and taboos.

Young men in this context would have had a voice in the decision, but the decision for marriage would have been much more in the hands of the parents and patriarchs. If the rabbinic conversations are any indication (discussed in the next chapter), the will and wishes of the groom might have been considered with regard to *whom* he married. But, for most young men, there would have been no question of *whether* to marry.

CHALLENGES

If a married Jesus seems awkward or sacrilegious to us, could it be that we are projecting our ideal of romantic love onto an ancient personality? Could it also be that we are imagining Jesus in a world of individualism rather than collectivism? As we will see in the next chapter, it was not uncommon for a young man, emerging from puberty and never having pursued a romantic relationship, to find himself matched to a potential wife. This match would have been pursued by his parents and for the well-being of the entire clan. Marriage *was not* a decision made on the basis of "falling in love."

Conversely, we would do well to recognize that popular portraits of Jesus pursuing Mary Magdalene like a first-century Romeo are anachronistic. Novelist Nikos Kazantzakis imagined that Jesus wanted a "normal life," one wherein he could pursue the woman (or women) of his desire and settle down. Historian William E. Phipps imagined that Jesus' wife turned to a life of prostitution in a tale of love lost and regained.[23] Such imaginative reconstructions tell us much more about ourselves than they do about Jesus. If we are to come to an informed opinion about Jesus' marital status, we will have to train our imaginations to work in ways that might seem foreign to us.

FURTHER READING

Joseph N. Bell, *Love Theory in Later Ḥanbalite Islam* (Albany: State University of New York Press, 1979).

Joseph Blenkinsopp, *Ezra-Nehemiah: A Commentary; The Old Testament Library* (Philadelphia: The Westminster Press, 1988).

Magda Bogin, *The Women Troubadors: An introduction to the women poets of 12th-century Provence and a collection of their poems* (New York: W. W. Norton & Company, Inc., 1980).

Harry C. Triandis, *Individualism And Collectivism; New Directions in Social Psychology* (Boulder: Westview Press, 1995).

Marilyn Yalom, *How the French Invented Love: Nine Hundred Years of Passion and Romance* (New York: HarperCollins Publishers, 2012).

AVERAGE JOE

Concerning a man who loves his wife as himself,
who honors her more than himself,
who guides his sons and daughters in the right path and
arranges for them to be married near the period of their puberty,
Scripture says: And thou shalt know that thy tent is in peace.

– TALMUD, YEBAMOTH 62B

We can say with a high degree of confidence that many of Jesus' disciples were married. We can also say that at least some of Jesus' brothers were married. We think that Paul was not married (at least during his missionary career) because he thinks that this is worth mentioning. This confirms what historians know of marriage in Jewish antiquity. Marriage was the rule – indeed, it was so common that one might not ever find reference to a religious leader's wife. This "detail" was simply not considered noteworthy. Paul is an outlier to this cultural norm, and so his choice not to marry is noteworthy. Really, it is quite possible that Paul had been married at some point. It was not uncommon for women to marry directly after puberty and die before they reached twenty-five years of age.[1]

In the previous chapter, I suggested that marriage in Jesus' culture would not have been the result of two people falling in love. I also suggested that the decision to marry would have been made for the good of the clan, not merely for the two people concerned. That said, the burden of finding the right match would have been primarily in the hands of two people: the fathers of the groom and bride. It is also important to recognize that the benefits of a good marriage would be enjoyed by two primary people: father and son. In Jesus' culture, as with many ancient societies, the most important relationship in the clan was that of the father and son. With this in mind, I will focus here on the kinds of motives and considerations that Jesus' father might have had. I will also discuss matters related to the average age of marriage in Jewish antiquity and the average life expectancy. These will be important considerations if we assume that Jesus was about thirty years of age when he began his public career as a preacher.[2] I will also suggest that Joseph probably lived to see his son reach puberty – that is, he lived long enough to be burdened with the responsibility of finding Jesus a wife.

I consider the sociological evidence put forth in this chapter to be the best argument for a historical wife of Jesus. This chapter will not offer the final word, but I think it does offer a few reasons to take the possibility seriously.

JESUS, SON OF JESUS

In the centuries after Judaism and Christianity parted ways, the Jewish rabbis evolved in a few different directions. Amid this diversity of Jewish thought, we have records of rabbinic conversations that took written form in at least two distinct times and places. These are commonly referred to as the Jerusalem and Babylonian Talmuds. Both these conversational threads discuss marriage at length.

The Babylonian Talmud, taking final written form in Babylon (modern-day Iraq, around 600 c.e., but also stemming from earlier times), tells us that the ideal age for men to marry was quite young by modern standards. Consider this conversation:

> Rabbi Huna was behaving according to his own saying when he said: "A man of twenty who has not married spends all

his days in sin" . . . So too it is taught by the school of Rabbi Yishmael: "Up to twenty years, the Holy One – blessed be He – sits and watches for a man, when he should marry a wife. When his twentieth year arrives and he has still not married, He says, 'May his bones blow away.'" . . . Rabbi Ḥisda said, "I desired more than my colleagues to marry at sixteen. Had I married at fourteen I could have said to Satan, 'An arrow in your eye!'"[3]

For the Babylonian rabbis, marriage was the only acceptable outlet for sexual desire. Developing a sexual identity outside of marriage was dangerously close to sin. For this reason, marrying young was virtuous. Here we see that the age of twenty was the upper limit for marriage. In such conversations, we hear the ages eighteen and twenty repeated often. Singleness beyond the early twenties was seen as a pressing problem.

It should also be noted that the standards for rabbis and regular people might have been different. This Babylonian Jewish conversation reflects a deep concern for focus on religious study without sexual distractions. Marriage directly after puberty, some thought, would tame a young man's sex drive. Conversely, some Babylonian rabbis believed in celibacy, arguing that a wife might distract them from religious study. In general, though, common men were closer to the ideal when they married young.

In many cases, the Babylonian rabbis are too far removed from first-century Judea to represent the values of Jesus' contemporaries. But, in this case, the value placed on early marriage may well represent a longstanding ideal. From before the Babylonian exile (c. 600 B.C.E.) to the writings of the Babylonian rabbis (c. 600 C.E.) there were those within Judaism who thought that marriage directly after puberty was ideal.[4] But, as I will discuss below, we must remain very cautious when applying rabbinic ideals to first-century life.[5]

The ideal of early marriage is probably directly related to life expectancy. Measuring life expectancy in the ancient world is a tricky business, but a few general claims can be made. Judging from over three hundred census returns from Roman-occupied Egypt, we estimate that the average life expectancy was between twenty and thirty years. This number is skewed, however, by high infant-mortality rates. One in three babies died within the first year of life. One in two children did not live past ten years. If a child was fortunate enough to live to age ten, her/his chances of living to forty were roughly 60 percent. She or he would have a 50 percent chance of seeing the age of forty-five.[6]

These statistics, of course, cannot speak to individual lives. They can, however, suggest a general outlook – and such expectations would have impacted marriage customs. Marriage customs and progeny would have been an absolute must for the survival of the collective. If a father could not assume that his fifteen-year-old son would live past forty, early marriage would have the virtue of better ensuring children.

But not every period in the history of Judaism reflects this ideal. The Jerusalem Talmud, generally thought to have taken written form one hundred to two hundred years earlier than the Babylonian Talmud, complicates this generalization of early marriage. While the ideal ages of eighteen and twenty are commonly mentioned among the Jerusalem rabbis, it was not uncommon for men to marry closer to thirty. One rabbi suggests a range that caps at forty.[7] So the Jerusalem and Babylonian rabbis seem to differ on the ideal age of marriage.

Another difference between the two schools of rabbis is that the earlier rabbis seem to have no prominent supporters for celibacy. These rabbis viewed marriage as a way to become a civic contributor, and that this was good for the society at large. Financial and social well-being flowed from the marriage union. As we saw in the last chapter, the centrality of family for financial and social well-being was a value inherited from early Judaism. It is worth reiterating Carol Meyers' succinct assessment that "family was inextricably connected with its landholdings."[8] With respect to the motivation for marriage, the Jerusalem rabbis probably reflect a longstanding ideology. Securing a match for one's son (especially one's eldest son) was tied to economic security and the hope for continued security. One can see why a father might seek a match for his son sooner rather than later.

But do these conversations tell us anything about marriage ideals or practices during Jesus' time? In order to answer this, we will need examples closer to the first century. One example comes to us from the Dead Sea Scrolls. This library of texts represents religious conversations (and sometimes practices) of a Jewish group that existed prior to, contemporary to, and shortly after the time of Jesus. So the Dead Sea Scrolls provide a window into some Jewish beliefs and practices during the time of Jesus.

One of the fragments found among the Dead Sea Scrolls tells us that a young man who wants to join the group "must not approach a woman for sex before he is fully twenty years old, when he knows right from wrong." The text continues to describe the membership of a young man's potential wife: "With the marriage act she, for her part, is received into adult membership."[9] Again we see the age of twenty connected with marriage, but this time twenty seems to be on the lower end of the ideal.

It is also worth noting that this, again, shows only an ideal. This scroll is interesting nonetheless because it confirms that the ideal age held by the Jerusalem rabbis was known during the time of Jesus. More importantly, the age of twenty is explicitly given as the minimum. The group that collected (and authored) the Dead Sea

---

THE DEAD SEA SCROLLS

The Dead Sea Scrolls are a group of fragments and documents that were found in caves near the Dead Sea in the late 1940s and early 1950s. Many of these texts were early versions of the Hebrew Bible and visions of a coming apocalypse. Other texts discuss rules for living in a religious sect called the "Yahad." This group seems to have gathered documents from all over Judea (and perhaps beyond) and kept them in clay jars. They also authored many of the documents themselves. The geographical area where the scroll were found is called Khirbet Qumran, not far from the Dead Sea.

Scholars debate how common marriage was practiced in this community. It was once thought that this group was celibate as a rule. Indeed there is some evidence that celibacy was practiced. However, the text mentioned in this chapter, and the bones of women and children found at the archeological site, caution against any definitive statements about their marriage practices.

Scrolls is generally thought to be very suspicious of gentile culture. In this case, however, the group seems to reflect the common Roman practice of late marriage (mid-twenties to thirties). This fragment confirms what many scholars say of first-century Jewish culture: "men married for the first time in their mid-to late twenties."[10]

A more concrete example of marriage practices for the upper class comes to us from an archeological discovery in 1960. Archeologist Yigael Yadin unearthed a leather bag in a cave near the Dead Sea that contained personal and legal documents belonging to a wealthy woman named Babatha. One of these documents is a marriage contract between Babatha and her first husband. His name was

"Jesus, son of Jesus."[11] This Jesus, it seems, was about twenty years of age when he married Babatha.

These documents also confirm that many people during this period died between ages twenty and thirty. Death at around age thirty created greater chances for remarriage, polygamy, child-custody complications, and estate disputes for widows. Jesus, son of Jesus, seems to have died less than five years after his marriage, leaving Babatha one son (also named Jesus). This example simultaneously demonstrates the problems associated with later marriage and the reality that many Jews of upper-class status did not adhere to the ideal of teenage marriage. The legal documents of Babatha also show that many wealthy Jews of this period were beholden to Roman law. Babatha kept these documents (written in Greek) in order to appeal to the Roman authorities in matters of property and familial dispute. With this in mind, it is necessary to say a brief word about Roman society and law.

Jews during the time of Jesus lived within the social matrix of the Roman Empire. Many Jews struggled to maintain a distinct society within this matrix, but all Jews lived in relationship or reaction to Rome. During Jesus' time, many Romans lamented the rise of singleness and childlessness among their citizens. There was a move by some Roman officials to return to the "good old days" of traditional marriage and family. In response to the increased popularity of singleness and/or childlessness, Augustus (63 B.C.E.–14 C.E.) introduced laws that penalized celibacy and encouraged progeny.[12] It is probable that these laws were targeted at social elites, but they would have influenced the lives of all classes. Men between the ages of twenty-five and sixty were expected to sire children. Women were expected to produce children between the ages of twenty and fifty. These age ranges provide further evidence of a social norm in the first century. Young adults were expected to marry and produce children in their early twenties and these pressures increased (to the point of legal obligation) in their late twenties.[13]

It could very well be that poor Jewish families did not need legal pressures and incentives to encourage marriage and family. Perhaps many poor Jews practiced teenage marriage and prolific child production, as was the ideal from early Israel to the medieval rabbis. But whether or not Jesus' family was poor and traditional or wealthy and economically tied to Rome, there would have been strong social expectations for marriage and family.

WHAT'S IN A NUMBER?

Amid a wide variety of eras, places, ideologies, and classes, most Jews of the post-biblical period held the age of twenty as important. Why?

Many rabbis used the age of twenty to measure the upper limit of puberty. If a boy does not produce two pubic hairs by the age of twenty, he can be declared a "eunuch." If a girl does not produce two pubic hairs by this age, she can be declared "sterile." One rabbinic text claims, "All the same is a boy nine years and one day old and one who is twenty years old but has not produced two pubic hairs."[14] The point of agreement in these Jewish texts is that the age of twenty (most commonly) is when a man is mature enough for marriage. Most males would have reached marriage readiness long before twenty; twenty years probably represents the upper limit of marriage readiness.

Before returning this discussion to Jesus, one last point is crucial. Michael Satlow writes: "For Galilean Jews, according to the Palestinian Talmud, honor was more important than money. Few events held more potential for the transfer of honor than marriage."[15] The pressure on a father to find the proper match for his children must have been enormous. The pressure to find a match for his eldest son, the one who would eventually provide spiritual guidance and financial security for the entire family, might have no parallel in Western culture. If this marriage contract fails in a way that brings shame to the family, it might have long-term consequences for one's family in the community at large. With this in mind, it is easy to see the benefits for securing a match for one's children early. In Jesus' culture, "early" was probably close to twenty years old.

JESUS, SON OF JOSEPH

Jesus' first thirty years will always be a source of curiosity. Aside from brief details of Jesus' family, and that he is a craftsman from Galilee, we have very little to go on. Mary, the mother of Jesus, seems to be an important character in the story of Jesus' public career. We also, as seen above, hear mention of Jesus' siblings. But what of Joseph?

Matthew, Luke, and John all mention Joseph, but Mark (the earliest of the four biblical Gospels) never refers to him. Perhaps the fact that Jesus' brother is named "Joses" (a short form of the name Joseph) suggests that Joseph was a family name, but why is Joseph not listed alongside his mother and brothers in Mark? Most historians have speculated that Joseph died before Jesus began his public career (thus, before Jesus was about thirty). But is this argument well based?

It seems that some people claimed that Jesus was born out of wedlock or was foreign born. In the Gospel of John, Jesus' adversaries imply that Jesus' father is unknown.[16] This claim paints a picture of a Jesus who is not fully Jewish. Matthew's Gospel seems to be pushing back against similar accusations. Perhaps this debate about Jesus' legitimacy was due to Joseph's absence. But this will have to remain speculative. What we can say is that Jesus was considered by some to be illegitimate. There might be several reasons for this; the absence of Joseph being only one of them.[17]

There have been traditional debates about the family of Jesus. Some of these debates, emerging from the fourth century C.E., focus on the perpetual virginity of Mary, the mother of Jesus. Those arguing for Mary's lifelong abstinence claimed that Jesus' "brothers" were half-brothers or cousins. But the view held by most scholars is that Jesus had at least four brothers and at least two sisters. Unless one is committed to the doctrine of Mary's lifelong virginity, there is no reason to think that Jesus' brothers and sisters were anything other than the biological children of Mary and Joseph.

It is possible that Joseph died when Jesus was under the age of ten, but the most likely guess is that he lived at least long enough to see Jesus reach puberty. While Luke's story about the Jerusalem rabbis teaching the twelve-year-old Jesus is generally taken as legend, this story corroborates the claim that Joseph was alive long enough to see Jesus approach maturity. Luke writes that Jesus "grew and became strong, filled with wisdom, and the favor of God was upon him."[18] This suggests that Jesus was approaching maturity before Joseph's departure from the story. Taken by itself, Luke's statement is inconclusive. But taken alongside the fact that Joseph had at least seven children, it is reasonable to assume that Joseph was present for most (if not all) of Jesus' childhood.

If so – if Joseph lived to see his eldest son approach maturity, he would have probably sought to arrange a match. This does not mean that Jesus was married, but given what we know of the standard ages for marriage (twenty to thirty), it would have been a pressing concern. Moreover, because Jesus was the eldest, it would have been a pressing concern for the whole family. It is also worth noting that mothers might have been more active in the matchmaking process than our records show. Mary herself could have pursued a match for Jesus, if Joseph had already died. This is not to say that either Mary or Joseph took steps in this direction, but they would have certainly felt societal pressure to do so.

CHALLENGES

The New Testament does not tell us that Jesus was married. But it also does not tell us if he ever skipped a stone, or laughed, or learned to dance, or countless other things that would have been common to the human experience. Are we to conclude that Jesus never whistled a tune just because the Gospels do not say so?

It is entirely possible that Jesus married during his twenties and that the Gospels just do not provide this information. Perhaps it simply wasn't relevant for their portraits of Jesus. Perhaps he married and his wife died before Jesus became a public figure. Getting married was just a natural stage of life – it would have been remarkable if Jesus never experienced this stage. So, I would argue that our default position should be that he did skip stones, and whistle tunes, and that he did get married – unless we have good reason to think otherwise.

It just so happens that we might have a few good reasons to think otherwise. These will be addressed in the next chapter.

FURTHER READING

D.S. Browning and E.S. Evison (eds), *The Family Religion and Culture* (Louisville: Westminster John Knox, 1997).

James Francis, *Subversive Virtue: Asceticism and Authority in the Second-Century Pagan World* (University Park: Pennsylvania State University Press, 1994).

K.C. Hanson and Douglas E. Oakman, *Palestine in the Time of Jesus: Social Structures and Social Conflicts* (Minneapolis: Fortress Press, 2008).

Matthew Kuefler, *The Manly Eunuch: Masculinity, Gender Ambiguity, and Christian Ideology in Late Antiquity* (Chicago: The University of Chicago Press, 2001).

Tim Parkin and Arthur Pomeroy, *Roman Social History: A Sourcebook* (New York: Routledge, 2007).

Michael L. Satlow, *Jewish Marriage in Antiquity* (Princeton: Princeton University Press, 2001).

James VanderKam, *The Dead Sea Scrolls Today*, revised ed. (Grand Rapids: Eerdmans, 2010).

ALTERNATIVE LIFESTYLE

*I mean, brethren, the appointed time has grown
very short. From now on, let those who have
wives live as though they had none . . .
and those who buy as though they
had no goods.*

– THE APOSTLE PAUL

Our default position should be that Jesus was probably married before he was thirty, unless we have good reason to think otherwise. But default positions are not conclusions. In this chapter I will suggest a few reasons as to why we might think of Jesus as a sexual nonconformist.

Jesus was expected to marry. If he wasn't matched to a wife in his early twenties, the pressure would have been mounting by his late twenties. Jesus' marriage – especially if he was the eldest son – would have provided civic stability and honor for his family. He would have felt the pressure to become a social and economic contributor. Civic responsibility and marriage fit hand-in-glove in Jesus' culture. In this chapter I will refer to this network of religion, honor, economics, and family as "civic masculinity." I will offer evidence that Jesus preached an alternative to civic masculinity.

CIVIC MASCULINITY

Biblical scholar Susan E. Haddox, in her reading of Genesis, suggests four criteria for masculinity.[1] While there are different ways to exhibit masculinity, a typical, biblical male:

1. avoids being feminized (especially avoids excessive attachment to women);
2. displays virility and strength (including warfare);
3. acts with honor (including provision for family, especially women);
4. speaks with persuasiveness, wisdom, honesty.[2]

It might be interesting to examine how the biblical portraits of Jesus compare and contrast with these criteria.[3] Because of my present focus, I will highlight only her third criterion: manhood was defined, in large part, by one's ability to act with honor within the clan with special emphasis on economic integrity.

Honor, of course, is a well-known biblical ideal. Famously, the fifth commandment given to Moses is to "honor your father and your mother." Less famous is the second part of this verse: "honor your father and your mother, *that your days may be long in the land which the Lord your God gives you*."[4] Honoring one's parents is directly tied to land stewardship. In both the traditional narratives and practical realities of Jewish life, honor connected one's ancestral property rights to future generations of inhabitants. We should not reduce honor to property considerations, but there is a greater danger in forgetting this connection. Honoring one's family included commemoration, ritual, worship, and so on. But no less noble, and of paramount importance, was honorable stewardship of one's inheritance.

This notion of familial honor was common throughout the ancient world, and continues in many parts of the world today.

A model citizen in the ancient Mediterranean would honor the father–son relationship above all others. The bond between the father and the eldest son was the most important because it represented more than just the "nuclear family" – it represented the continuity between patriarchs and their ongoing (hopefully eternal) lifeblood through progeny. Jewish tradition honored this connection by keeping a portion of the ancestral land and wealth undivided as the joint possession of the extended family. While secondary heirs would receive portions of the inheritance, the eldest son would become the economic patron who would anchor the family's well-being.

The ideal eldest male in Greek society carried similar responsibilities as "he assumed the responsibility for the honorable marriage of the family's daughters; he acted as patron with the family by distribution of the father's patrimony to his male siblings and to the family's clients."[5] The Roman institution of "paterfamilias" mirrored this Greek ideal. This "father of the estate" managed the fortunes of the extended family and was responsible for the family's civic connection within larger society. While the ideal of civic masculinity normally envisions a father figure who presides over a grand estate, the impact of this ideal was veritably global and created expectations for men even in modest households.[6] One did not need to be a wealthy landowner, or even the eldest male of a clan, to feel the pressure of civic masculinity: "Corresponding to gender-specific space are gender-specific tasks and roles. Males are either engaged in agriculture or civic affairs (= 'outdoors' or 'public'); thus they are farmers, herders, traders, or civic leaders."[7] Civic masculinity was built on the premise that the ideal male would have the power and responsibility of ownership. However wealthy he was, he would wield authority over his people and possessions. In this way, the ideal civic male would contribute to the larger economic and social integrity of the nation.

In the matrix of Greek, Roman, and Jewish cultures, civic masculinity provided the continuity of family wealth, but it also provided a continuity of collective morality. So integral was the family to Roman society that a first-century trend toward celibacy was seen as a national threat. As I mentioned in the previous chapter, Caesar Augustus introduced laws to penalize celibate citizens. Celibate males were prohibited from inheriting wealth and property from their next of kin. Married couples without children were obligated to release as much as half of their inheritance to kinsmen with children, or to the state.[8]

Augustus imposed these laws to preserve traditional marriage and family, put into place when Jesus was a child. Tacitus, a Roman politician and historian, wrote that these laws did little to squash the trend among social elites.[9] What these laws show, however, is that the ideal of civic masculinity was a norm that (according to some) needed defending against the alternative lifestyle of celibacy. While on the rise, celibacy was considered by many to be a lifestyle set against the common good. This lifestyle would have been equally (perhaps even more) subversive for traditional Jewish families in Roman-ruled Israel.

Choosing celibacy in Jesus' culture would have been as aberrant as choosing to not have a bank account in modern Western culture. Such an odd choice would demand some sort of explanation. Worse – and this is where the bank-account analogy fails to convey the full consequences – this decision would have had ramifications for mothers, siblings, and extended family members. For an eldest son to choose a lifestyle contrary to civic masculinity would have been seen as a dishonor to patriarchs and a willful neglect of future generations.

GODLY EUNUCHS

The Gospel of Matthew includes one of the most peculiar sayings in the New Testament. Jesus addresses the topic of men who differ from sexual normalcy:

> For there are eunuchs who have been so from birth, and there are eunuchs who have been made eunuchs by others, and there are eunuchs who have made themselves eunuchs for the sake of the kingdom of heaven. Let anyone accept this who can.[10]

This saying is notoriously perplexing. Taken at face value, Jesus addresses masculinity. But does he also imply gender more generally? It is unclear whether Jesus is talking about a simple absence of penis and/or testicles or whether he is talking about a gender principle that might extend to women as well as men. You may recall that some rabbis saw fit to declare a boy a "eunuch" if he had not produced two pubic hairs by the age of twenty. Is Jesus referring to stunted maturity and/or sterility? I would argue that this saying has much more in view than just physical deformity. To this end, I will make four observations.

My first observation is that Jesus acknowledges that both nature and choice are involved in this identification. Some people are simply born with a physicality that differs from sexual norms. Others choose an alternative lifestyle. I think that the conversation that leads up to this saying helps to explain what Jesus is talking about: Jesus' disciples say, "It is better not to marry." Jesus confirms, "Not everyone can accept this teaching, but only those to whom it is given."[11] It is a conversation about singleness that leads to Jesus' statement about eunuchs. At least in Matthew's context, being a eunuch is not simply about lacking reproductive organs, it implies a lifestyle choice: celibacy.[12] Those who choose the life of a eunuch are choosing to forgo the traditional avenues of marriage and family.[13]

Second, there can be no doubt that this statement would have undermined civic masculinity for those who knew the instructions of Deuteronomy: "He whose testicles are crushed or whose male member is cut off shall not enter the assembly of the Lord."[14] From this perspective, becoming a eunuch is a subversion of the Jewish ideal for civic masculinity. Even if Jesus is simply talking about mere physical deformity, this particular deformity would have had civic disadvantages.

Third, Jesus thinks that choosing this sexual alternative can be done for godly reasons. Jesus clearly states that some men choose this as a godly alternative. The choice to forgo fatherhood and traditional masculinity is not necessarily contrary to God's purposes. Indeed, Jesus says here that some choose this alternative lifestyle for the sake of "the kingdom of Heaven." Given that marriage was woven together with social and economic security, Jesus' suggestion that a man might choose otherwise for godly reasons is both socially and fiscally subversive.

Fourth, whatever our interpretation of this passage, we must acknowledge that Jesus is saying something scandalous. Jesus says that "not everyone can accept this teaching, but only those to whom it is given." He then makes his statement about godly eunuchs and concludes with these words: "Let anyone accept this who can." Clearly Jesus knew that this saying would be hard to hear for many people – he says so twice. Jesus expects that people with traditional views of fatherhood and masculinity are going to have a hard time accepting this teaching.

In today's climate of gender advocacy, it is common for scholars to "oversex the text." It would be typical for those invested in social activism to turn Jesus into a modern advocate. I would suggest that we must be cautious when our Jesus begins to look too much like us. But it is equally irresponsible to tame Jesus – to smooth over his words in favor of a traditional view of sexuality and gender. In the case of eunuchs, Jesus is clearly challenging a first-century view of civic masculinity.

SECURITY IS FOR THE BIRDS

Jesus' saying about godly eunuchs is just one indication among many that Jesus discouraged traditional notions of civic masculinity. This short section will list a number of Jesus' sayings as they are found in the Gospels. In providing this list, I am not making any judgment about whether these are word-for-word citations from the lips of Jesus. What I hope to show is that Jesus left the general impression that his views on marriage and family did not follow societal expectations for civic stability.

Consider this exchange between Peter (who represents the disciples) and Jesus:

> Peter said, "See, we have left our own and followed you." And Jesus said to them, "Truly I say to you, there is no one who has left house or wife or brothers or parents or children, for the sake of the kingdom of God, who will not receive many times as much at this time and in the age to come, eternal life."[15]

I must confess that I find this saying to be among the most troubling in the New Testament. Did Jesus encourage his disciples to leave their families behind? Did the men who followed Jesus become irresponsible husbands and fathers? Did they leave their dependants in the lurch? In a culture of collectivism, such a teaching would have had enormous economic and social consequences.[16] Jesus knew well the costs. His disciples remembered these words:

> Do not think that I have come to bring peace on earth; I have not come to bring peace, but a sword. For I have come to set a

man against his father, and a daughter against her mother, and a daughter-in-law against her mother-in-law. And a man's foes will be those of his own household. He who loves father or mother more than me is not worthy of me; and he who loves son or daughter more than me is not worthy of me.[17]

In Luke's Gospel, this sentiment is even more troubling: "If anyone comes to me and *does not hate* his own father and mother and wife and children and brothers and sisters, yes, and even his own life, he cannot be my disciple."[18]

These words ring hollow in the Christianized West. In a culture where those most invested in Jesus' teachings are the same people who tend to champion "traditional family" values, these are hard words to hear and even more difficult to render into religious practice. But among the earliest Christians, these words were commemorated and cherished. Many people who joined Jesus' movement found themselves detached from their families. This meant that many were cut off from their social and financial support networks. These words legitimized an alternative view of marriage and family.[19] It seems that Jesus redefined "family" for his followers:

While he was still speaking to the people, behold, his mother and his brothers stood outside, asking to speak to him. But he replied to the man who told him, "Who is my mother, and who are my brothers?" And stretching out his hand toward his disciples, he said, "Here are my mother and my brothers! For whoever does the will of my Father in heaven is my brother, and sister, and mother."[20]

In this passage, Jesus redefines family as those who are bound by religion over and against blood relations. To many of Jesus' audiences, the distinction between religion and household responsibilities would have seemed counterintuitive. Like many modern religious people, most of Jesus' contemporaries would have seen good religion, good family, and good citizenship as vines intertwined. But Jesus seems to want to drive a wedge through societal norms.[21] It is also crucial to notice that Jesus models his teaching by belittling (dishonoring?) his own family. His scandalous redefinition of family is exemplified in his own life.[22] In a similar vein, Luke provides this exchange:

> While Jesus was saying these things, one of the women in the crowd raised her voice and said to him, "Blessed is the womb that bore you and the breasts at which you nursed." But he said, "On the contrary, blessed are those who hear the word of God and observe it."[23]

The early Christians used these words to unify themselves as a spiritual family.

Traditionally, scholars have argued that new Jewish "converts" to Christianity were ostracized from their families and from their larger social and business networks. But I think this idea has missed an important element. I think that it is likely that Jesus' first Jewish followers were encouraged to disassociate from their blood relatives. Many of these followers found themselves cut off from their social and economic networks because they chose to disavow traditional honor, economic, and family values. Furthermore, there is good reason to believe that this practice stems from Jesus' preaching. This exchange between Jesus and two would-be followers illustrates my point:

> . . . a scribe came and said to him, "Teacher, I will follow you wherever you go." Jesus said to him, "The foxes have holes and the birds of the air have nests, but the Son of Man has nowhere to lay his head."[24] Another of the disciples said to him, "Lord, permit me first to go and bury my father." But Jesus said to him, "Follow me, and allow the dead to bury their own dead."[25]

Notice again that Jesus uses himself as a model. He calls himself the "son of man" and explains that he has "nowhere to lay his head." This, of course, is hyperbole. Jesus probably slept in many different locations, including the houses of followers and patrons. What Jesus suggests here is that he has forsaken the home of his family. This would have been seen by many as a disregard for the command to "honor your father and your mother."[26]

Both of these would-be followers are forced to count the cost of discipleship. Following Jesus meant surrendering economic and social security. The scribe is told that becoming a follower involves the sacrifice of stable bedding and roofing. The disciple in this passage is told to abandon his responsibilities as a biological son. This, of course, would also mean sacrificing any claim he might have on inheritance. Set together, both conversations probably spoke against traditional notions of religion, honor, economics, and family – what I have called civic masculinity.

This is not to say that every follower of Jesus disavowed his or her family, but there is a great deal of evidence that the earliest followers of Jesus forsook civic masculinity, including marriage and family.[27] The problems that this must have created for the biological families of the first Christians must have been enormous. Perhaps this is why Jesus' disciples eventually returned to the practice of marriage, as assumed by Paul.

Jesus' stance on wealth and his indictments of the wealthy are well known. His famous "consider the lilies . . . consider the birds . . ." sayings are lofty aspirations in the Christianized West. Jesus preached, "do not worry about your life, what you will eat or drink; or about your body, what you will wear."[28] But in a culture where honorable men promoted the social and economic securities of their families, such a message would have castrated would-be fathers and husbands. Without possessions and the power to provide for a family, influence society, and propel honor to future generations, men could not honor their fathers, much less support wives.

CHALLENGES

In the Introduction, I suggested that John the Baptist lived like an ascetic, forsaking all worldly comforts. Jesus, on the other hand, did not live like an ascetic. The reason that Jesus could feast, drink, and attend parties was because he was willing to accept patronage from wealthy followers. But, having forsaken his home in Galilee, Jesus would have had a very difficult time establishing himself as a civic entity.

Marriage allowed men to become socially and fiscally secure within civil society. Yet Jesus is remembered for criticizing social and fiscal security. Jesus, it seems, had an altogether different notion of family. So while our default stance should expect that Jesus was probably married, the Gospels give several indications that he might not have been the marrying type. He did not seem to hold blood ties in high regard. He did not choose a lifestyle that would provide for a household. He seemed to live as if the world as he knew it was coming to an end. Thus provision for future generations was not a part of his message. In all of these ways, Jesus subverted civic masculinity and quite possibly the institution of marriage, which stood at the center of civic masculinity.

For these reasons, I think that it is highly unlikely that Jesus was married to Mary Magdalene or to any of his followers during his preaching career. We cannot rule out the possibility that Jesus was previously married (perhaps in his early twenties), but he seems almost "anti-family" during his teaching and preaching career. I have argued that civic responsibility and marriage fit hand-in-glove in Jesus' culture. Jesus seems to have rejected traditional notions of civic responsibility. Does this suggest that he chose the aberrant and alternative lifestyle of celibacy?

FURTHER READING

Colleen Conway, *Behold the Man: Jesus and Greco-Roman Masculinity* (Oxford: Oxford University Press, 2008).

Ovidiu Creangă (ed.), *Men and Masculinity in the Hebrew Bible and Beyond; Bible in the Modern World 33* (Sheffield: Sheffield Phoenix, 2010).

Anthony Le Donne, *Historical Jesus: What Can We Know and How Can We Know It?* (Grand Rapids: Eerdmans, 2010).

Dale B. Martin, *Sex and the Single Savior: Gender and Sexuality in Biblical Interpretation* (Louisville: Westminster John Knox Press, 2006).

Stephen D. Moore and Janice Capel Anderson (eds), *New Testament Masculinities; Semeia Studies 45* (Atlanta: Society of Biblical Literature, 2003).

BRIDE OF CHRIST

For your Maker is your husband, the Lord of hosts is his name;
the Holy One of Israel is your Redeemer, the God of the
whole earth he is called. For the Lord has called you like
a wife forsaken and grieved in spirit, like the wife of
a man's youth when she is cast off, says your God.

– THE BOOK OF ISAIAH

The Christianized West is in the business of creating Jesus in our own image. Look no further than Bill O'Reilly's latest book: *Killing Jesus: A History*.[1] O'Reilly, a politically conservative television personality, has co-authored a history of Jesus' execution that portrays him as a proto-libertarian. Given the evidence presented in the previous chapter of this book, O'Reilly's reading of Jesus is dubious at best. Again, we are reminded that portraits of Jesus can and do reflect the agendas and biases of the artist. But no portrait of Jesus is entirely fabricated. For all of his evolution in the various cultural commemorations of him, there are aspects of Jesus that remain constant throughout the ages – not static, but highly difficult to change. Every new evolution of Jesus (if it isn't entirely rejected by the culture) is somewhat continuous with the last. Two thousand years of cultural evolution can easily turn Jesus from an anti-wealth iconoclast to a proto-libertarian. This is why professional historians are keenly interested in a figure's immediate impact. In other words, how was Jesus remembered and commemorated immediately after his death?

Crucial to any historical reconstruction is the question of impact. What Jesus' followers did after he was gone can tell us a great deal about the impact he had. After all, Jesus was one of the most (if not the most) influential figures in history. We should expect that his followers discussed, debated, and adapted his teachings in whatever new social circumstances they found themselves. This chapter will attempt to bridge Jesus' historical impact with my previous discussions of second- and third-century Christianities. This will help us answer the question, "How did the Church become convinced that Jesus was celibate?" Finally, I will return to the medieval period to discuss how the concept of the "bride" of Christ continued to evolve during the time of the troubadours.

My previous chapter suggested that Jesus might have promoted a very odd version of Jewish collectivism. If Jesus did challenge his followers to rethink the fundamental elements of honor, family, and economics, we should expect that early Jewish-Christian groups struggled to find symmetry and a sense of normalcy. Below I will suggest that the impact of Jesus' alternative vision of civic masculinity can be seen in various currents of the Jesus movement.

In Jesus' absence, first-century followers encountered several different kinds of resistance and internal conflict. The attempt to adapt the "Christian" economic and social vision of community pushed different groups in different directions. Some groups attempted to incorporate traditional family units within these communities. Others took on more ascetic personalities. And, to extend the argument of my previous chapter, these various attempts to develop and adapt Jesus' teachings were tied to ideas about economic collectivism. The idea of "the bride of Christ" emerged from these developing struggles to find economic and social identity.

JESUS THE UTOPIAN GROOM

Scholars call theories of the last days "eschatology." Among Christian theologians, this tends to be connected with the belief of a final creation of a "New Heaven" and a "New Earth." This particular doctrine was adapted from Judaism. Indeed, during Jesus' time, this eschatology was a popular point of discussion and debate. In almost every form of ancient Jewish eschatology, there was a hope that the Lord would return as the divine Judge. This belief was an answer to a long history of injustice. The chaos of the past could not be changed, but you could hope that your fathers and their fathers would someday see justice on the last day. On that day, the Lord would return to reward and punish as his divine wisdom dictated.

Within this paradigm, it was imperative to continue the lineage of your forefathers and honor their traditions. As discussed over the last few chapters, the institution of civic masculinity symbolically connected the lifeblood of one's ancestors to future generations. This long vine was rooted as deep as Abraham and extended as far as the last days. Many believed that the righteous dead would be brought back to life and reunited on that final Day of Judgment. On that day, all religious persecution would end and all of the sons of Israel lost to war and slavery would be reunited in a kingdom of purity and peace. If you lived within this system, you owed it to your ancestors and to future generations to live with honor until that day came.

But what if you earnestly believed that you would see the great Day of Judgment during your lifetime? What if you believed that Jesus predicted the imminent coming of the new world order with these words: "Truly, I say to you, there are some standing here who will not taste death before they see the son of man coming in his kingdom."[2] Would this change the way you thought about securing prosperity for future generations?

New Testament scholar Dale B. Martin writes: "Jesus' rejection of the traditional family and his creation of an alternative community signaled the imminent, or perhaps incipient, in-breaking of the kingdom of God." Martin argues that Jesus taught his followers to forsake the institutions of marriage and family and "enter into an alternative, eschatological society." He continues: "The household was part of the world order he was challenging. It, along with other institutions of power, would be destroyed in the coming kingdom. The household, moreover, represented traditional authority, which he was challenging at every turn."[3]

Many Christians believed that they were living in the last days. Their alternative community, in preparation for the Day of Judgment, meant the end of the typical household structure. As suggested in chapter 8, this new world order was a subversion of economic power structures – what I have termed civic masculinity. Why build wealth for the future when the "kingdom of God" is close enough to taste?

As odd as this might sound, Jesus' belief that his movement was inaugurating the last days might explain his view on food and wine. In a saying that contrasts Jesus from his contemporaries, Mark writes:

> Now John's disciples and the Pharisees were fasting; and people came and said to him, "Why do John's disciples and the disciples of the Pharisees fast, but your disciples do not fast?" And Jesus said to them, "Can the wedding guests fast while the bridegroom is with them? As long as they have the bridegroom with them, they cannot fast. The days will come, when the bridegroom is taken away from them, and then they will fast in that day."[4]

In this passage, Jesus draws an analogy between himself and a groom: "The historical Jesus may have made an indirect claim with this saying to be the chief agent of God and thus to mediate the presence of God in the last days."[5]

If this saying does represent Jesus' expectations for a "New Earth," it suggests that he drew from the prophetic visions of Israel as a bride/wife in Hebrew scripture.[6] God's role as the masculine provider is often symbolized by an abundance of food.[7] It could be that feasting was important to Jesus and his followers because it symbolized God's utopian household. Whatever the case, this saying represents a reaffirmation of the symbolic masculinity – and therefore *provision* – of God.

The Lord of Israel is the ultimate patron; Jesus' understanding of God is as his "Father" and "King." Such metaphors implied the Lord's provision for his family. Perhaps, then, Jesus' "groom" analogy bespoke a wedding feast that brought his followers into a divinely ordained economy. This economy was marked by provision enough for all family members. It is no coincidence that the Gospel of John inaugurates Jesus' public career in the setting of a wedding feast.[8] If Jesus' message had been taken seriously, there would have been no room in Christianity for a single dominant male (or lineage of males) who provided for the rest – they were collectively and equally "the bride."

It was not long, however, before Jesus himself became the ultimate patron in the minds of his followers. Even though Jesus undermined traditional notions of civic masculinity, his followers would soon extend and expand the metaphor of him as a groom.[9] It is not surprising then that Christianity eventually projected traditional notions of civic masculinity onto Jesus (I will return to this theme below).

It is absolutely crucial that we do not lapse back into our twenty-first-century understanding of courtship when we read this passage. If Jesus called himself a "groom," this would have brought to mind images of sexual consummation, but only secondarily. The primary responsibility of the husband is to be a patron, a provider. If Jesus wanted to convince people that the justice of God and the utopia of Israel were imminent, what better way to communicate this than to celebrate with feasting and drinking?

THE WEDDING AT THE END OF THE WORLD

A counterbalance to Jesus' message of alternative masculinity is found in the book of Revelation. This apocalyptic Jesus echoes some of the Gospels' ambiguity about masculinity, but overshadows this ambiguity with a definitively masculine Jesus.

THE BOOK OF REVELATION

Revelation (also called the Apocalypse of John) is the final book of most New Testaments. It reads much like other "apocalyptic" texts from this period. The author provides a series of visions that reveal heavenly realities that are believed to mirror historical events, events contemporary with the author, and also future events. In the case of the book of Revelation, it includes seven letters (each to a different city's church) followed by several visions. Many of these visions represent events contemporary with the book's authorship in the first century. In other words, much of this book is a political commentary that provides hope for Christians at the height of the Roman Empire. Key to this hope is the return of Jesus, who will eventually subdue the forces of evil and rule over a New Heaven and a New Earth.

The Jesus of the Apocalypse is a slain lamb, which is dubiously masculine by almost every measure. This lamb, however, is risen and victorious. Jesus is thus lionized, a king, a warrior, an impaler, a conqueror, a groom. As Jesus' portrait becomes increasingly masculine, the metaphor of the Church as "the bride" becomes increasingly important. These early Christians, male and female, are designated as a woman who has "made herself ready" for her husband on her wedding day.[10]

This might explain why one of our earliest depictions of Jesus is erotic.[11] But before I speak to this eroticism, I must reiterate that concerns for *provision* are primary with the groom/bride metaphor. We should not allow our preoccupations with sexual images to eclipse the more important economic theme. More on this theme below.

The Ghent Altarpiece: Adoration of the Mystic Lamb (c. 1425), Jan (and Hubert?) van Eyck. This tempera-and-oil on panel is sometimes called the greatest masterpiece of the Northern Renaissance. This particular panel recalls John's climactic vision from the book of Revelation. In this vision, the lamb symbolizes Jesus who was slain (i.e. crucified) but is now victorious and glorified.

Many scholars have noted the parallels between the following passages. The first is from the erotic poetry of Song of Songs; the second passage is from Revelation:

> I slept, but my heart was awake / Hark! My beloved is knocking "Open to me, my sister, my love / my dove, my perfect one"[12]

> Behold, I stand at the door and knock; if any one hears my voice and opens the door, I will come in to him and eat with him, and he with me.[13]

The concepts of "knocking," the lover's "voice," and "opening" echo one of the most sexually suggestive images in Hebrew poetry. The poem in Song of Songs continues:

> I have taken off my dress / How can I put it on again? / I have washed my feet / How can I dirty them again? / My beloved extended his hand through the opening / And my feelings were aroused for him. / I arose to open to my beloved / And my hands dripped with myrrh / And my fingers with liquid myrrh / On the handles of the bolt. / I opened to my beloved . . .[14]

Here the poet plays with the metaphor of a "door" or a "gate" that serves as an anatomical euphemism. This is just foreplay, however, as the male lover does not consummate the union. For all of the emphasis that is placed on the "opening" (repeated four times), the lover does not enter.

It is likely that the author of Revelation (called "John") is echoing this metaphor from Song of Songs. The book of Revelation also emphasizes "door" imagery, and the divine caller also stands only at the opening, not entering.[15] The key difference between John's imagery is that the beloved community in the book of Revelation 3:18–19, is not yet ready for the wedding banquet. The divine caller finds his beloved lacking in the proper clothing for the occasion.

We will eventually learn that pure clothing is a symbol for displays of harmonious relationships.[16]

While the casual reader of the book of Revelation might miss the conjugal symbolism in chapter three, all doubt is removed in chapter nineteen: ". . . the marriage of the Lamb has come / and his bride has made herself ready / it was granted her to be clothed with fine linen, bright and pure."[17] At the climax, the bride's readiness is shown by her spotless wedding dress. So we see that the unconsummated love of chapter three is resolved in chapter nineteen. Finally, the divine caller of chapter three promises to share a meal with his beloved community. In chapter nineteen, we learn that this meal is called "the wedding feast of the Lamb."[18] The author of the book of Revelation is clearly playing with the image of a wedding union between bride and groom.

This long-awaited wedding feast symbolizes the final reconciliation and consummation between Jerusalem and her God. It should also remind us of the famous imagery in Song of Songs: "He brought me to the banqueting house / and his intention toward me was love."[19] In sum, the imagery of conjugal celebration became a potent metaphor of the early Christians. When John imagined the return of Jesus, he called himself, his brothers, and his sisters "the Bride." In this vision, Christ becomes the sole provider for the household of God.

Finally, while much more should be said about John's idealized and demonized women, I will take this opportunity to speak to the reality behind the symbols.[20] The chief obstacle between Jesus and the beloved community of the book of Revelation, chapter three, verses fourteen to twenty-two, is that they are rich and apathetic. The statements "I am rich, I have prospered, and I need nothing" and the indictment that they are "lukewarm" should be contrasted with the early and widespread Christian ideal of economic equality. In the book of Revelation, chapter three, the divine caller desires to provide a meal for the beloved community. Provision, of course, was the primary responsibility of the husband. In this way, Jesus became the divine patron in the minds of his followers.

The earliest followers of Jesus shared their wealth and strove to live in a community of equals.[21] They failed miserably at times, but they shared poverty and wealth in their attempt to become the "bride" of Christ. Their belief that Jesus was their heavenly husband was incarnated in their efforts to care for the poor and destitute. The elevation of Jesus meant the systematic demotion of the apathetically wealthy. This ideal can be seen throughout the New Testament, but it almost always betrays how difficult it was for various groups to achieve cohesion.

Paul commanded Christians to share poverty and wealth so that "there may be equality."[22] Paul, much like the author of the book of Revelation, hoped that economic, social, and theological unity would transform a wealthy, apathetic, and theologically divided people into "a pure bride."[23]

THIS JESUS, THAT JESUS

In chapter 1, I alluded to a second-century Christian named Tatian. According to Christian theologian Irenaeus (writing in the second century), Tatian "composed his own peculiar type of doctrine . . . he declared that marriage was nothing else than corruption and fornication."[24] It is difficult to know how well Irenaeus represents Tatian's view, but Clement (*c.* 150–*c.* 215) is probably refuting a "heresy" of this ilk when he writes:

> There are those who say openly that marriage is fornication.
> They lay it down as a dogma that it was instituted by the devil.

> They are arrogant and claim to be emulating the Lord [Christ] who did not marry and had no earthly possessions. They do not know the reason why the Lord did not marry. In the first place, he had his own bride, the Church. Secondly, he was not a common man to need a physical partner. Further, he did not have an obligation to produce children; he was born God's only son and survives eternally.[25]

The argument and counterargument provided by Clement represent a discussion about Jesus' marital status. This debate emerged one hundred years after the death of anyone who might have known Jesus in his early years. Furthermore, I do not think that either argument reconstructs Jesus' motives with any plausibility. But the logic of their arguments notwithstanding, I think that this debate provides an interesting window into the common assumptions of two dissonant schools of early Christianity.

Given Jesus' odd teachings about marriage and family, one can easily see how some might conclude that he promoted a kind of asceticism. It is also easy to see the logic behind Clement's view: Jesus, as an eternal being, did not need to extend his life through progeny. Both arguments, while flawed, assume that there was no literal wife of Jesus. *This Jesus* was celibate for reason A; *that Jesus* was celibate for reason B. But both this Jesus and that Jesus are presumed celibate.

And here we return to the question of a literal wife of Jesus. Because both arguments assume Jesus' celibacy as a fact, the perception of a celibate Jesus must have existed prior to the debate itself. Therefore it is probably safe to say that there was a widespread belief in the early second century that Jesus had been celibate. Pushing to the roots of both assumptions – thus moving closer to the first century – both Tatian and Clement address Jesus' famous "eunuchs saying." It seems that different interpretations of

Matthew 19, resulted in different approaches to marriage and family (or at least, different justifications for common practices).

Clement also frequently appeals to Paul's Letters to the Corinthians to make his case for Christian marriage. Clement quotes Paul when he writes:

> Hence Paul speaks against people who are like those I have mentioned, saying: "You have then these promises, beloved; let us cleanse ourselves from all defilement of flesh and spirit, perfecting holiness in the fear of God." "For I am jealous for you with a divine jealousy, for I betrothed you to one husband to present a pure virgin to Christ." The Church cannot marry another, having obtained a bridegroom; but each of us individually has the right to marry the woman he wishes according to the law; I mean here first marriage.[26]

Simply put, Clement is arguing that "betrothal" to Christ is a collective and spiritual reality and should not negate the individual and physical marriages of believers. Elaine Pagels is probably correct to suggest that Tatian had previously argued that those married to Christ should not forsake this monogamy by marrying themselves to a human partner.[27] If so, both Tatian and Clement make their cases by appealing to Matthew and Paul. Thus, neither second-century theologian demonstrates any knowledge of Jesus' early adult life concerning a wife of Jesus. The only information that they have about the life of Jesus comes from his public career as a preacher. This adds further support to my argument that Jesus was probably not married during his public preaching career. It does not rule out the possibility that Jesus had been married previously.

Bringing this conversation to the present, I have often heard modern Christians echo (without knowing it) Clement's logic: Jesus was not married because Jesus was not normal. Statements like this may well be correct, but are probably based on faulty assumptions.

In my experience, when Christians say that Jesus was "not normal," they generally mean that Jesus was too holy for marriage and, by implication, sex. What I have suggested in this book is that Jesus seems quite abnormal in his teachings about honor, family, and economics. When due attention is given to Jesus' teachings on these subjects, we are in a position to critique common Christian assumptions about a possible wife of Jesus. Christians, like Clement, might have been correct about Jesus' celibacy during his public ministry, but for the wrong reasons. Interestingly, the imagined Jesus of politically conservative circles has allowed Christians to promote a non-sexual Jesus but ignore his teachings about honor, family, and economics.

Before concluding, I will showcase a story that stands almost equidistant between Jesus' world and ours. This is a story of a Christian who attempts to embody Jesus' teachings.

ROMANCING FRANCIS

The following is a story based on tradition, probably more truth than fiction.

In the early thirteenth century, there was a playboy who whiled away his days entertaining the wealthy kids of Assisi. He entertained them with his wit, song, and marshal demonstrations. He wooed their approval with food and drink. Squandering the opportunities given him, Francis of Assisi didn't excel as a student. Rather, he was interested in the performance arts of the troubadours. And while he was well situated to become a wealthy cloth merchant like his father, he showed no interest in the family business. He did, however, revel in the latest fashions, so clothing was important to him after all. Of course, Francis met the expectations of the time and crusaded off to war against the Islamic infidel.

And then he got sick. Illness is the great leveler, striking the rich and the poor alike (and this was even truer in the Middle Ages). It was then that Francis received his first vision in the form of a dream. Preoccupied with his military career, Francis interpreted his dream to mean that he would be a great conqueror. With renewed vigor Francis continued his crusade to win further glory and a few more blows against the armies of Islam.

He took ill again and received a second vision. This time he was told by a voice to return to Assisi. He became changed, visibly sullen, taking no pleasure in parties. Francis was adrift and refused to be consoled. When asked if he thought to marry, he finally revealed what he had been stewing on: "Yes," Francis replied, "I am about to take a wife of surpassing fairness." To the surprise of his rich friends, brothers in arms, and hopeful parents, this bride was not a woman of flesh and blood, but an ideal. The woman of surpassing beauty was "Lady Poverty."

Like many young people who find religion, Francis ran as far as he could from his pre-conversion life. In the months that followed, St. Francis emptied his wallet and forsook his family fortune in an attempt to live out the utopian vision of Christianity. Francis gave up the wardrobe he once prized and expressed his new life ethic with a coarse tunic and a rope around his waist.

What is often forgotten about St. Francis is that he was a very accomplished preacher in his time. It was his sermons that attracted a rich, young woman named Clare to be "married to Christ." Much like Francis's conversion, Clare forsook her family's wealth and took a vow of poverty. By 1219, the first and second orders of St. Francis had been established, the second of which would eventually be called the "Poor Clares."

In light of my discussion of early Christian communities of shared poverty and wealth, the metaphorical parallel between the "marriages" of Francis and Clare are telling. Francis describes his conversion much as a troubadour would romanticize an elite lady. Indeed, the story of Francis's wooing of "The Lady Poverty" was told as something of a love story.[28] In his choice to walk "unshod" like Christ, Francis throws himself into his new religious life like a lovesick troubadour.[29] In this way, he endeavors to "take a bride . . . Lady Poverty." Interestingly, we see the "bride of Christ" metaphor adapted to suit the romantic preoccupations of thirteenth-century Italy.

Clare, on the other hand, becomes "married to Christ." Notice the difference in metaphor. Francis marries an allegorical woman who embodies the lifestyle of Jesus. Clare marries a masculine persona. But, despite the difference in metaphor, both conversions looked much the same in practice. Almost twelve hundred years after Jesus' preaching, the ideals of economics and marriage are still inexorably entwined.[30] Both Francis and Clare understood the metaphorical Christian "marriage" to include both celibacy and poverty.

In the year 1221 (although that date is not certain), St. Francis was preaching to a congregation in Camara, Italy. They were so moved by his preaching that the entire congregation wanted to join his order. The only problem was that they were regular folk; many were married or served a necessary function within the city. It would have been unwise to sell their homes because they were needed at home. St. Francis then instituted his "Third Order" – what is now called "The Brothers and Sisters of Penance." Rather than encouraging the all-or-nothing lifestyle that he lived, the Third Order was meant to be a middle space between the monastery and the city.

I think that the idea of a Third Order is worthy of reflection – not for its eventual rules, but for its initial impetus. In a world where becoming "married to Christ" meant asceticism, isolation and (all too often) misogyny, Francis made a profoundly progressive move by allowing married men and women to participate as the bride of Christ while married to each other. Francis knew that vows of poverty stand in antithesis to familial care. As enamored as Francis was with poverty and celibacy, he was willing to create sacred space for those who were committed to their families, land, and cities.

The Western world was changing during the time of Francis and his troubadour friends. Romantic love had become a social force. Courtship was *en vogue*. In order for the "bride" metaphor to extend into this shifting culture, it evolved in meaning and practice.

CHALLENGES

In sum, the assumption that Jesus was celibate emerged from interpretations of (1) his teachings about civic masculinity, and (2) the metaphorical title "bride" when applied to the Church. Both of these interpretations begin in the first century and are probably connected with Jesus' eschatological outlook.

The "bride of Christ" is a collective; it is a socio-economic ideal; it is an intimate, spiritual consummation of religious experience. In these ways, the metaphor builds a bridge between us and the Jesus of public memory through the perceptions of early believers. If we want to answer the question of Jesus' marital status, we will be forced to contend with Jesus' social and economic message of collectivism.

Lastly, we see a shift in marriage practices in the medieval period. This resulted in an adaptation of the metaphor "bride of Christ." St. Francis of Assisi first romanticized and then faced the real-world concerns of shared poverty and wealth. Should we see Francis's "Third Order" as a dulling of Jesus' alternative lifestyle? Or was Francis incarnating Jesus' inclusivity? Perhaps both are equally true. Marriage, after all, is about compromise.

FURTHER READING

Dale C. Allison Jr., *Jesus of Nazareth: Millenarian Prophet* (Minneapolis: Fortress, 1998).

David Aune, *Revelation; Word Biblical Commentary* 52a (Waco: Word Publishers, 1997).

Marianne Blickenstaff, *"While the Bridegroom is with them": Marriage, Family, Gender and Violence in the Gospel of Matthew*, Library of New Testament Studies (Edinburgh: T & T Clark, 2005).

Kate Cooper, *The Virgin and the Bride: Idealized Womanhood in Late Antiquity* (Cambridge: Harvard University Press, 1996).

Frank J. Matera II, *Corinthians: A Commentary: New Testament Library* (Louisville: Westminster/ John Knox, 2003).

Augustine Thompson, *Francis of Assisi: A New Biography* (Ithaca, NY: Cornell University Press, 2012).

10

WAS JESUS MARRIED?

*"It is a narrow mind which cannot look at a subject
from various points of view."*

– GEORGE (MARY ANNE EVANS) ELIOT

I am well aware that many of my readers will have picked up this book to see what I have to say about a literal wife of Jesus. While the topics covered in these pages have been much broader in scope, I have tried to offer my best arguments for and against the possibility of a married Jesus. This chapter will offer a summary of these arguments and tie together several threads that have run throughout. My hope is that I can provide a clearer picture of my answer to the question "Was Jesus married?".

If you skipped ahead to read this chapter first, shame on you and bless you! Shame on you for your impatience, and bless you for skipping all of the sordid and scandalous stories revealed over the course of this book. You've missed my reading of the pillow talk between Jesus and Salome. You've missed my discussion of ritual kissing between Jesus and Mary. You've missed my take on the recently publicized *Gospel of Jesus' Wife*. You've missed my analysis of Jesus the polygamist and the gay Jesus. Shamefully and happily, you've missed my argument that Jesus offered a subversive alternative to "civic masculinity." This book, in large part, has been about ancient and modern attempts to project sexual identities onto Jesus.

Much of what follows in this chapter will rely on the research put forth in chapters 6 through 9 of this book. By way of warning, if you have not followed my explanations of collectivism, civic masculinity, and eschatology, my summary here might be hard to follow. Nevertheless, this chapter will draw together the key themes of the second half of this book.

THE CASE FOR A HISTORICAL WIFE OF JESUS

Historians of ancient cultures and figures must not succumb to the desire to fill in every gap left by historical memory. In keeping with one of the key themes of chapters 2 through 4, sometimes the problem of silence must remain a problem. Conjecture can damage the very legacies that we hope to commemorate. In keeping with one of the key themes of chapters 3 through 5, there is always the risk of projecting our own agendas and aspirations onto the figures of Jesus and Mary Magdalene.

As a case in point, there is very little we can say with confidence about Mary Magdalene. What of her family? What of her social status? If she was among the wealthy supporters of Jesus' mission, does this imply an elite social standing? I cannot make any such claim with confidence. A historical fiction from the thirteenth century may portray Mary Magdalene as a wealthy princess, but I must take that for what it is: *fiction*. Even if some of our early evidence hints that Mary might have been wealthy, there is still no warrant for making such a claim.

Mary's social status is an example of a particular point of data that defies any confident assertion. But not every gap in historical memory is of this ilk. Some gaps can be filled in – with confidence – without specific data. Sometimes, historical memory is fortified by our knowledge of common practices within a society.

For example, consider the question: *Was Jesus breastfed?* It might seem like an odd query, but it is relevant to this chapter in multiple ways. Its primary relevance is that it is a query that can be answered positively without any data specific to Jesus. Indeed, while the nursing Madonna became prominent in fourteenth-century Italy,[1] historians have very little data on this particular point of fact that is

Nursing Madonna (*c.* sixteenth century), artist unknown. One of the hallmarks of renaissance portraiture is the realism of Mary and Jesus. Whereas previous periods depicted the child Jesus as a little adult with unrealistic proportions, from the 1400s onward he is depicted with infant features. Although the features of this portrait are somewhat out of proportion (i.e. not quite realistic for an infant), the fact that Jesus is nursing conveys the concern for the humanity of both mother and child during this period.

specific to Jesus. The *Proto-Gospel of James* portrays the infant Jesus breastfeeding. In this narrative, Jesus "went and took the breast from his mother Mary."[2] But, of course, this second-century text is a historical fiction and cannot be read as history (in our usual sense of that genre).

The Gospel of Luke contains this exchange between Jesus and a woman who called out from his audience:

> One of the women in the crowd raised her voice and said to him, "Blessed is the womb that bore you and the breasts at which you nursed." But he said, "On the contrary, blessed are those who hear the word of God and observe it."[3]

The *Gospel of Thomas* conveys a related conversation:

> In the crowd a woman says to him: "Blessed is the womb which bore you and the breast which fed you!" He said to her: "Blessed are those who have heard the word of the Father and keep it! In truth, days are coming when you will say: Blessed is the womb that has not brought forth and those breasts which have not given suck!"[4]

In my view, this saying very plausibly reflects Jesus' downplay of blood relationships and biological progeny. In other words, this conversation cannot be reduced to mere fiction; it reflects history. Here the anonymous woman assumes that Jesus was breastfed and (indirectly) blesses Mary, his mother. Even so, assumptions do not always represent historical facts. Jesus does not confirm or deny her assumption. Even if he did, should we imagine that Jesus remembered his own infancy?

In the case of the question "*Was Jesus breastfed?*" our earliest and best sources do not convince us of any fact specific to Jesus. But we can conclude, on other grounds, that Jesus was, in fact, breastfed.

This we can claim as historical fact for the simple reason that socio-typical study tells us so.[5] We should imagine that all first-century Galilean children who survived infancy were breastfed, unless we have reason to think otherwise. There is no reason to think that Jesus was an exception to the rule in this case. It is, then, ironic that the fictional portrait in the *Proto-Gospel of James* of Jesus being nursed conveys a historical probability. In spite of its genre – that being fiction – it corroborates a historical fact. Here I underscore a matter of historical method: we tend to fill in the gaps. While novelists do so with the tools of fiction, historians do so with the tools of sociology, anthropology, archeology, and so on. We can arrive at historical facts based on what we know of common practice in a given culture.

The question *Was Jesus married?* is very much like the question *Was Jesus breastfed?* The two questions are not perfectly analogous, but the comparison might be helpful to convey how foundational marriage actually was for Jesus' culture and religious integrity. To underscore a key theme of chapters 6 and 7: marriage was a cultural given. It was ubiquitous. It was seen as a foundational element of honoring one's parents and the lifeblood of one's ancestors. It was a path to economic integrity and manhood. Marriage was considered necessary for the survival of one's people in a culture where the survival of one's people was the highest ideal, the greatest good. We should imagine that almost every first-century Galilean who lived to age thirty was married, unless we have reason to think otherwise. Both breastfeeding and marriage were practiced to ensure survival.

Awkward as it might seem to us in the Christianized West, our default setting has been wrong. Our default setting has been to assume that Jesus was celibate because he was too holy for sex. But most people in Jesus' culture would have considered celibacy to be altogether unholy. Multiple rabbis recite and comment on a sermon called "In Praise of a Wife":

> There are twelve good measures in the world, and any man who does not have a wife in his house who is good in her deeds is prevented from enjoying all of them. He dwells without good, without happiness, without blessing, without peace, without a help, without atonement, without a wall, without Torah, without life, without satisfaction, without wealth, without a crown.[6]

While the form of this sermon postdates the time of Jesus, the sentiments of the sermon are quite ancient. Marriage was a path to holiness, it was an avenue to civic contribution and economic stability, and it was a way to extend the lifeblood of one's patriarchs into the future. In Jesus' culture, honor was bound to marriage and family. Indeed, the first divine blessing and command to humanity implies marriage and progeny. God instructs the man and the woman, "Be fruitful and multiply."[7] As an extension of God's fruitfulness in creating, the creatures made in the divine image are commanded to be fruitful in progeny. This fundamental feature of Judaism made marriage a given for holiness and (oftentimes) a requirement. Some rabbis instructed men to find a match for their sons while the father's hands were "still on the neck" of their sons.[8] The practice of early matchmaking allowed the father to receive honor by extending the longevity of his family (and of Israel at large) through his sons.

While this ideal does not *necessarily* reflect the thinking of Jesus' parents, it reminds us that Jesus was subject to the will and wishes of his family when he was young. We should be aware that Jesus' parents would have been expected to find a wife for him. Jesus' thoughts about his marital status would have been only one factor in a family decision. For the sake of illustration, it would be much more likely that Jesus was married in early adulthood and that his wife died in childbirth (as was all too common); it would be far less likely that he would have dishonored his father and mother and rejected the Abrahamic blessing of progeny.

If the New Testament was truly silent about Jesus' sexuality, our most cautious move would be to settle at the default setting. Given no further clues about Jesus' views on marriage and family, we would be compelled to conclude that Jesus was married based on socio-typical practice.

JUDAISM AND JESUS

I must say a word about Jesus' lifelong commitment to Judaism and the well-being of the Jewish people. My argument against a married Jesus is primarily found in chapter 8 of this book, where I demonstrate how strange Jesus' views on marriage, family, honor, and economics must have seemed to his kinsfolk. Moreover, I suggest that Jesus' lifestyle would have run contrary to some very foundational Jewish beliefs and practices. I did not foresee such an unexpected turn in my research when I began writing this book. I am surprised that the Jesus revealed to me in my research has, at times, seemed so "anti-family."

So I reiterate a point that I made in chapter 1: in Jesus' day there was a wide variety of Jewish expressions. The fact that Jesus challenged some of these expressions does not make him any less Jewish. In fact, it probably situates him quite comfortably within the line of Jewish prophets and wisdom teachers. I have no doubt that some of his contemporaries accused him of being an outsider and a foreigner, but the earliest followers of Jesus – those who knew him best – knew that he was from *and for* the people of Israel.

The historical Jesus does not transcend or outmode the religious expressions of Israel. I think Jesus knew that his teachings about marriage and family were subversive, but he did not think of himself as "anti-Jewish." For that matter, I doubt that he saw himself as "anti-family." My perspective, no doubt, is limited by my own cultural categories, and the category "anti-family" is probably an egregious misstep. At the same time, I can only see with my own eyes.

I will offer one more point along these lines. Many of Jesus' subversive statements about masculinity, economics, progeny, and so on, would have scandalized most gentiles in the ancient Mediterranean. Romans who continued to support the marriage and family incentives of Caesar Augustus would have been especially scandalized by Jesus' teachings. If Jesus was an iconoclast, he was a Jewish iconoclast first and foremost.

THE CASE AGAINST A HISTORICAL WIFE OF JESUS

In chapter 7, I observe that the age of twenty is an important transitional point for Jewish men concerning their readiness for marriage. I suggest that most first-century Jewish men were married between the ages of twenty and thirty. This emphasis on the ideal age (while not always indicative of practice) seems to survive into the rabbinic period. While the rabbis vary in their instructions, the chief virtue of the age of twenty was that it represented the upper limit of puberty.[9] Jesus' parents would have probably started to consider a marriage for Jesus soon after this transition.

What I did not discuss at length was the rabbinic significance of the age of thirty. This list of "life stages" is probably too late to offer much help, but it will assist in illustrating an important point:

- At 5 years old one is fit for the Scripture,
- At 10 for the Mishnah,
- At 13 for the fulfilling of the commandments,
- At 15 for the Talmud,
- At 18 for the bride-chamber,
- At 20 for pursuing a calling,
- At 30 for authority,
- At 40 for discernment,
- At 50 for counsel,
- At 60 to be an elder,
- At 70 for grey hairs,
- At 80 for special strength,
- At 90 for bowed back,
- At 100 a man is as one that has already died.[10]

At first glance, this list seems to confirm what we generally assume about ideals for marriage shortly after puberty. The two-year gap between the bride-chamber (age eighteen) and pursuing a calling (age twenty) suggests that a young man would live with his bride within his parent's house even before he was ready for the demands of full-fledged adulthood.

But a closer look at this list reveals two things that caution us against any definitive argument on the basis of life stages. First, notice how idealized and generalized these numbers are. After the age of eighteen, these stages are represented in generic decades. Second, as discussed in chapter 7, studies of life expectancy suggest that very few people lived past sixty years. Are we to imagine that there were so few qualified elders? Probably not.

The better solution is to see these numbers as symbolic.[11] The ages of thirty, forty, fifty, and sixty are symbols of maturity of mind. Perhaps they were seen as milestones, as they are understood in many cultures, but they are not to be taken literally. We should not read this list and imagine that people would literally obtain "discernment" ten years after they obtained "authority," or that their hair wouldn't grey earlier than age seventy.

If so – if life stages were generally symbolic – the Gospel of Luke's general assertion that Jesus was "about thirty" may well be symbolic.[12] Perhaps Jesus was closer to his mid-twenties, and Luke simply means to convey that Jesus was ready for authority. Conversely, Jesus may have been in his early to mid-thirties. This qualification is important because any argument about Jesus' marital status based on typical marriage practices and typical marriage ages must remain tentative without a firm assertion of Jesus' age.

If we are cautious, no firm conclusions can be drawn concerning Luke's motives for the generality "about thirty." Likewise, we should be cautious not to give too much weight to the assumption that Jesus was close to the upper limit of marriage expectations. It would be safe to say that Jesus was firmly within the marriage-age range when he began his preaching career, but we cannot say exactly how old Jesus was when he began his subversive teachings about marriage and family.

This is where the analogy with the question "*Was Jesus breastfed?*" must be qualified. We can say with confidence that Jesus was an infant and was nourished like an infant. Jesus would have had no choice in this. He would, however, have had more to say about a potential marriage match (although the will and wishes of the young man should not be overstated). Marriage, like mother's milk, was a cultural given, and the burden of survival would have been on the shoulders of the parents of the clan. But, in Jesus' time and place, we do have precedents for celibacy.[13]

Striking to the heart of the matter, we cannot say *when* Jesus first decided to downplay the importance of what I have termed "civic masculinity" (biological family, economic responsibility, religious continuity related to land ownership, and so on). Could it be that Jesus inherited his nonconformist views of civic masculinity from John the Baptist? The Gospel of Luke portrays the preaching of the Baptist like this:

> He said therefore to the multitudes that came out to be baptized by him, "You brood of vipers! Who warned you to flee from the wrath to come? Bear fruits that befit repentance, and do not begin to say to yourselves, 'We have Abraham as our father'; for I tell you, God is able from these stones to raise up children to Abraham."[14]

In Luke's portrait, John the Baptist commands his audience to birth the metaphorical fruits of repentance to prepare for judgment day. Is this metaphorical bearing of fruit to be heard in contrast to literal childbearing? Did the Baptist mean to say that the biological fathers and sons of Israel were as unimportant as rocks? Or did he mean to say that the fathers and sons of Israel were defined by the land, not owners of the land?[15] Whatever the case, John the Baptist seems to be challenging a traditional understanding of patriarchy and progeny.

Did Jesus grow up in a traditional household, with traditional views of marriage and family, until he met John the Baptist? Perhaps it is impossible to disentangle the influence of Jesus, the Baptist, and the Lukan editor in our accounting of this unique ideology. Who influenced whom is a question that must remain open-ended.

What can be asserted with confidence is that Jesus was remembered for his nonconformity concerning marriage and family.

As seen above, Jesus was remembered for saying something along these lines: "In truth, days are coming when you will say: Blessed is the womb that has not brought forth and those breasts which have not given suck!"[16] Even if Jesus never phrased the sentiment in exactly these terms, this saying fits well with the general impression that he left.

The Jesus we find in the Gospels had a very strange interpretation of "honoring" of one's father and mother. I will here set together a variety of sayings (some of which have been discussed in chapter 8). Again, I'm more interested in illustrating the general impression left by Jesus:

> "If anyone comes to me and does not hate his own father and mother and wife and children and brothers and sisters, yes, and even his own life, he cannot be my disciple."[17]

> Another of the disciples said to him, "Lord, permit me first to go and bury my father." But Jesus said to him, "Follow me, and allow the dead to bury their own dead."[18]

> And when they saw him they were astonished; and his mother said to him, "Son, why have you treated us so? Behold, your father and I have been looking for you anxiously." And he said to them, "How is it that you sought me? Did you not know that I must be in my Father's house?"[19]

> And a crowd was sitting about him; and they said to him, "Your mother and your brothers are outside, asking for you." And he replied, "Who are my mother and my brothers?" And looking around on those who sat about him, he said, "Here are my mother and my brothers!"[20]

> And Jesus said to [his mother], "O woman, what have you to do with me?"[21]

These statements and others like them are found in the Gospels of Matthew, Mark, Luke, and John and suggest that Jesus valued his eschatological mission over and against his own family relationships. Given the social implications of such a subversive stance, many of Jesus' contemporaries would have thought him insane. Indeed, when Jesus brought his new "family" of disciples to his hometown, his family "went out to seize him, for people were saying, 'He is beside himself.'"[22] In this portrait, Jesus looks to be the sort of son who brought shame upon his biological family.

These (sometimes embarrassing) impressions of Jesus indicate that he acted independently from the wishes of his family, particularly his parents. So when the Gospel of Luke and the *Gospel of Thomas* depict a woman calling out, "Blessed is the womb that bore you and the breasts at which you nursed,"[23] and depict Jesus contradicting this blessing of Mary, we are given further evidence that Jesus had a strange idea about what it looked like to honor one's parents.

According to Luke, Jesus says, "On the contrary, blessed are those who hear the word of God and observe it."[24] This saying conveys a feature characteristic of Jesus' teaching: the true family of God is tied together not by blood but by faithfulness to the instructions of Israel's scriptures.

This might seem an ironic statement coming from Jesus. As I discussed in chapter 8, Jesus seems to have an awkward relationship with Moses' fifth commandment: "Honor your father and mother . . ." But perhaps the key here is the emphasis on *metaphoric* family. If Jesus' "true family" is his eschatological community, he cannot be accused of dishonoring his biological father and mother. If this reading is close to the mark, Jesus may well have brought shame upon his biological family (from one perspective) yet still thought of his mission as honorable.[25]

The *Gospel of Thomas* appends this statement to Jesus' contradictory blessing: "Blessed is the womb that has not brought forth and those breasts which have not given suck!" This dubious blessing probably reflects Jesus' view of final judgment. Jesus' mission seems to have been focused on the return of God as judge and a final utopia. This "blessing" of barren wombs and breasts might reflect Jesus' belief that God's judgment is very near. But what is most telling is that Jesus has not rendered this teaching in the form of a curse.

For example, the prophetic book of Hosea proclaims the curse of "no birth, no pregnancy, no conception!" The prophet asks the Lord to give the indicted people a "miscarrying womb and dry breasts."[26] In a culture where progeny meant survival and honor, such a curse would be heard as a death sentence – and, even worse, a fatal shaming.

For Jesus to call barren wombs and breasts a "blessing" indicates a subversive notion of family and honor. Recalling my argument in chapter 8, Jesus' subversion of "civic masculinity" suggests that he was the rare example of a Jewish religious leader who encouraged celibacy. It could be that Jesus' vision of Israel's utopia did not include marriage. When Jesus was asked about this by fellow Jews who did not believe in life after death, Jesus said that people who rise from the dead "neither marry nor are given in marriage, but are like angels in heaven."[27] In the Gospel of Luke, Jesus says:

> The sons of this age marry and are given in marriage; but those who are accounted worthy to attain to that age and to the resurrection from the dead neither marry nor are given in marriage, for they cannot die anymore, because they are equal to angels and are sons of God, being sons of the resurrection.[28]

In proclaiming that the heavenly rule of God was close enough to touch, Jesus began to enact certain symbols that pointed to his prophetic vision. He promoted eschatological feasts, formed a spiritual "family," and he (most likely) forsook literal marriage in favor of his mission. This may well provide us with the necessary context for his praise of "eunuchs who have made themselves eunuchs for the sake of the kingdom of heaven."[29] Jesus encouraged his followers to accept this teaching, knowing that it would have seemed a subversion of the norms of civic masculinity. As I have argued in chapter 8, Jesus' subversive message about marriage and family was part and parcel of his teaching about economic and patriarchal honor systems:

> Peter said, "See, we have left our own and followed you." And Jesus said to them, "Truly I say to you, there is no one who has left house or wife or brothers or parents or children, for the sake of the kingdom of God, who will not receive many times as much at this time and in the age to come, eternal life."[30]

In short, our earliest and best sources for the life of Jesus do not give us the portrait of a teacher who instructed men to become civic patrons. Given all of this evidence, the pertinent question remains: *Did Jesus practice what he preached?* I think that he probably did.

This, of course, does not prove that Jesus was unmarried before his preaching career. It does, however, make it very difficult to imagine that he was married to Mary Magdalene or to any of his followers. In his career as a religious leader – short-lived as it was – Jesus was a sexual nonconformist. Specifically, he had invested in the two-sided coin of economic disobligation and celibacy.

CHALLENGES

In my introduction and chapter 1, I surveyed the evolution of Christian thinking about Jesus' sexuality. As misogynistic and fear-driven notions of sexuality evolved, the sexual identity of Jesus devolved. The second-century ascetics, I argued, arrived at a celibate Jesus with weak reasoning. Their ascetic Jesus – the Jesus who never defecated, left footprints, or wed – was a fiction of their own projections. While they may have been unwittingly correct about Jesus' marital status, their rationale was illegitimate.

We in the Christianized West inherited our iconic Jesus from Christian asceticism. And here we arrive at an irony too thick to ignore: even though our assumptions about Jesus were wrong all along, we were unwittingly close to the right answer about Jesus. The celibate Jesus of our iconographic imagination was a fiction. But, in spite of ourselves, we were probably right about Jesus' marital status, at least concerning his public career.

This little book is just one step along the way toward a better solution. The quest for the wife of Jesus will be ongoing and will produce a variety of conclusions. On this point I am certain. But perhaps some of the talking points raised in this book will serve as a guide for future historical constructs.

While this might seem an anticlimax for a book titled *The Wife of Jesus*, I would challenge my readers to remember that the "why" questions of history are just as important as the "what" questions. Jesus was not celibate because sex is sinful or because the Church has claimed status as the wife of Jesus. If true – if our most celebrated and despised icon was celibate for other reasons – we in the Christianized West will do well to reconsider our misogynistic and fear-driven notions of sexuality. Perhaps our notions of civic masculinity will become causalities on our continued quest for the wife of Jesus.

Afterword

PORTRAITS AND MIRRORS

Women have served all these centuries as looking-glasses . . .
Whatever may be their use in civilized societies, mirrors are
essential to all violent and heroic action.

– VIRGINIA WOOLF

In the Introduction I wrote that no historical Jesus book is just about an ancient "him" – or, in this case, an ancient "her and him." This book is indeed about the possibility of a wife of Jesus, but it is just as much about us: the Christianized West.

We have been in the business of creating Jesus in our own image for a long time. We have created Jesus as a romantic groom, a gay advocate, and a polygamous Mormon. We inherited Mary as a repentant prostitute (itself a fiction) and replaced that image with the image of a royal bride. In each of these portraits, we find reflections of the emerging aspects of ourselves. Here we arrive at one of the most important elements of any quest for the wife of Jesus: the search for Jesus' wife involves playing with our own reflections. Oversexing the text of the *Gospel of Philip*, letting our collective imaginations run wild over Mary Magdalene, forging documents to fuel our media appetites – these are all indications that the quest for the wife of Jesus reveals our own obsessions and insecurities.

One could hardly reveal this truth better than Nikos Kazantzakis. He writes:

> Struggle between the flesh and the spirit, rebellion and resistance, reconciliation and submission, and finally – the supreme purpose of the struggle – union with God: this was the ascent taken by Christ, the ascent which he invites us to take as well, following in his bloody tracks.

The author, made famous by his scandalous portrayal of Jesus, then reveals his motives: "If we are to be able to follow him we must have a profound knowledge of his conflict, we must relive his anguish." Clearly, Kazantzakis was motivated by his own inner conflict. He felt that he could best follow the bloody tracks by reliving Christ's anguish. In this way, Kazantzakis attempts to gain the "profound knowledge" of Christ's suffering by suffering himself. One must ask, "Was Kazantzakis illuminating or projecting his own angst in his portrait?" Perhaps both. Either way, we the audience are witnessing Kazantzakis' angst in Jesus' image. He claims that Jesus "conquered the invincible enchantment of simple human pleasures." Is this true? Kazantzakis seems convinced that it is:

> Temptation – the Last Temptation – was waiting for him upon the Cross. Before the fainted eyes of the Crucified the spirit of the Evil One, in an instantaneous flash, unfolded the deceptive vision of a calm and happy life. It seemed to Christ that he had taken the smooth, easy road of men. He had married and fathered children . . . But all at once Christ shook his head violently, opened his eyes, and saw . . . He had not married, had not lived a happy life.[1]

Kazantzakis concludes that Christ "reached the summit of sacrifice: he was nailed upon the Cross. Content, he closed his eyes. And then there was a great triumphant cry: It is accomplished!"[2]

Or, in fewer words (but no less telling) Kazantzakis wrote, "My entire soul is a cry, and all my work the commentary on that cry."[3] It is clear that in his *The Last Temptation of Christ* Kazantzakis was telling the story of his own struggle through historical fiction. His dehumanizing portrayal of Mary was a casualty in his wrestling match with God. What Kazantzakis really wanted was an angst-ridden – and therefore relatable – Jesus. Mary Magdalene's portrayal as a prostitute who had lost her faith served his narrative to this end. Mary was just a prop to help humanize Jesus. Mary became the framing that Kazantzakis wanted in order to create the Jesus he needed.

This is not far from what the Gnostic Christians were doing when they wrote their fictions of Salome and Mary. It also recalls the Mormon creation of an ancient witness to Christ's polygamy. It is less important that we agree or disagree with any of these portraits; it is more important to recognize our deep-seated need to question our own sexual insecurities with answers about Jesus.

I do not for one moment think that Jesus' cry from the cross had anything to do with a temptation to wed and settle down. But Kazantzakis was not trying to tell the history of Jesus, he was trying to reconcile himself with Jesus. Similarly, our fascination with the so-called "Gospel of Jesus' Wife" tells us much more about ourselves than it does about Jesus.

The quest for the wife of Jesus is thus a struggle for reconciliation. Kazantzakis was trying to reconcile "the flesh and the spirit" in his struggle to find "union with God." These are metaphors that we project in order to create sacred space for ourselves.

We find in the Christian story the archetypes of Father, Son, and Spirit. We find the metaphors of "Brother" and "Beloved" in the New Testament. Catholic tradition has given us the archetypes of "Blessed Mother" and "Virgin." These archetypes and others have infused Western civilization with a Christocentric psyche. In other words, Jesus remains a cultural force of gravity in our religious, social, political, and media-oriented lives. And yet, Christianity has always had an awkward relationship with sexual types. Is it any wonder that we're preoccupied with sex?

It was only a matter of time before we began a new quest for the wife of Jesus. We need the archetype of "Wife" as much as we need those other types. But our ancient texts will never reveal enough to convince us, and our modern scandals will always be too tempting to resist. As long as we project our insecurities onto our portraits of Jesus, we will continue to stare at our own uncomfortable reflections. We will continue to peep, like an anxiety-ridden Willem Dafoe, through that all-too-thin veil – begging for reconciliation and settling for spiritual voyeurism.

Notes

Introduction

1. Paul, one of the earliest Christians, claims that he has freedom to live like the rest of the apostles. He claims that he should be able to accept financial support, to eat and drink, and to marry. These three practices seem to be linked as signs of a "normal" lifestyle. Paul's choice to be temporarily celibate will be discussed elsewhere in this book. My point at present is that sex, food, and money were ideologically linked in the cultures of John the Baptist, Jesus, and Paul. Their relationship will be discussed more thoroughly throughout this book.

2. Dale B. Martin, *Sex and the Single Savior: Gender and Sexuality in Biblical Interpretation* (Louisville: Westminster John Knox Press, 2006), p. 97.

3. Luke 7:33–34.

4. Bill Watterson, *Homicidal Psycho Jungle Cat: A Calvin and Hobbes Collection* (Kansas City, Mo.: Andrews McMeel Publishing, 1994), p. 152.

5. Excerpt from Yosef Hayim Yerushalmi, *Zakhor: Jewish History and Jewish Memory* (Seattle: University of Washington Press, 1982), reproduced in *The Collective Memory Reader* (eds J. Olick, V. Vinitzky-Seroussi, and D. Levy) (Oxford: Oxford University Press, 2011), pp. 206–207.

Chapter 1

1. Quoted from Cathleen Falsani, *The Dude Abides: The Gospel According to the Coen Brothers* (Grand Rapids: Zondervan, 2009), p. 111.

2. For more on the image and influence of James Bond see Judith Roof, "Living the James Bond Lifestyle", in *Ian Fleming and James Bond: The Cultural Politics Of 007* (eds Edward P. Comentale, Stephen Watt, and Skip Willman) (Bloomington: Indiana University Press, 2005), pp. 71–86.

3. Hal Childs, *The Myth of the Historical Jesus and the Evolution of Consciousness* (SBLDS 179; Atlanta: Society of Biblical Literature, 2000), p. 98.

4. Chris Keith, *Jesus' Literacy: Scribal Culture and the Teacher from Galilee* (London: Bloomsbury, 2011), pp. 165–187.

5. For more on the God of the Hebrew Bible in relation to other ancient Israel theologies see April D. DeConick, *Holy Misogyny: Why the Sex and Gender Conflicts in the Early Church Still Matter* (New York: Continuum, 2011), pp. 1–14.

6. For the sake of space and focus, I will not detail the many and varied permutations of ascetic expression during this period. I should acknowledge that the term "encratism" (pertaining to self-discipline) is probably more fitting for some of the examples that I will discuss in this book. I will stick with the word "asceticism" to avoid undue jargon. In sum, I tend to see degrees of asceticism in Platonic thought, Gnosticism, and Jewish mysticism. In what follows I will be speaking of asceticism very broadly. The reader should be aware that there are some important differences between these categories that cannot be addressed here. But, generally speaking, most Greek education between 100 B.C.E. and 200 C.E. (what could be called "Middle Platonism") adopted or adapted some form of dualism between the physical world and higher realities. As is always the case with neighboring ideologies, some expressions developed as reactions to previous expressions. But, in general, asceticism is the attempt to move closer to a higher reality and farther from the material world.

7. Prov. 5:18–19 (New American Standard Bible).

8. From Galen's lost commentary on Plato's *Republic* cited and translated in R. Walzer, *Galen on Jews and Christians* (London: Oxford University Press, 1949), p. 15.

9. Paul's marital status will be discussed later in this book. At present, it is worth noting that Paul may well have been married at some point in his life.

10. In this film, the protagonist's journey leads him into a hedonist party where he demonstrates that he is all but disinterested in sex. "The Dude" passes out and literally sleeps through the party and into the next stage of his journey. Filmmaking duo Ethan and Joel Coen are quite fond of retelling ancient stories like this one.

11. St. Jerome, *On Marriage and Virginity*, 22.19.

12. Augustine, *On Marriage and Concupiscence*, 1.4.

13. Augustine, *On Marriage and Concupiscence*, 1.5.

14. St. Thomas Aquinas, *Summa Theologica*, 153.2.

15. Quoted by Clement of Alexandria, *Stromateis*, 3.59; cf. also *Stromateis*, 3.7.

16. Clement of Alexandria, *Stromateis*, 3.49.

17. I will discuss this possibility further in chapter 9.

Chapter 2

1. Sandra Jacobs, "Divine Virility in Priestly Representation: Its Memory and Consummation in Rabbinic Midrash" in *Men and Masculinity in the Hebrew Bible and Beyond; Bible in the Modern World* 33 (ed. Ovidiu Creangă) (Sheffield: Sheffield Phoenix, 2010) p. 163.

2. Translations from the Chinese by Arthur Waley (New York: Alfred A. Knopf, 1941), pp. 72–73. I provide this poem to illustrate that the problem of the silence of women in history is not a specifically Jewish or Mediterranean one. I do not intend to suggest that these problems are identical from culture to culture, only that there is evidence of widespread and analogous phenomena.

3. Hu and Ch'in are two places separated by a great geographical distance.

4. I should acknowledge that if Fu Xüan is guilty of enclosing the voice of an ancient Chinese woman in his poem, I am equally guilty of enclosing this voice within these pages. Moreover, my cultural distance from this voice risks further alienation; compare Yak-Hwee Tan, "The Question of Social Location and Postcolonial Feminist Hermeneutics of Liberation" in *Feminist Interpretation of the Bible* (eds Silvia Schroer and Sophia Bietenhard) (London: Sheffield Academic Press, 2003), pp. 171–178. Gayatri Chakravorty Spivak's insights notwithstanding, I am convinced that

bridge building between disparate social placements is worth attempting, even if early attempts must be nuanced with the maturity of later generations.

5. However, see Tal Ilan, *Silencing the Queen: The Literary Histories of Shelamzion and Other Jewish Women, Texte und Studien zum Antiken Judentum* 115 (Tübingen: Mohr Siebeck, 2006); Kenneth Atkinson, *Queen Salome: Jerusalem's Warrior Monarch of the First Century* B.C.E. (Jefferson: Mcfarland, 2012).

6. Catholic tradition has long held that Joseph (the father of Jesus) had been previously married and had sired Jesus' "half-brothers" before he was betrothed to Mary, the mother of Jesus. This belief stems from the agenda to preserve the "perpetual virginity" of Mary. This is to say that many Catholics throughout the ages believed that Mary was a virgin her whole life. Therefore, the fact that Jesus had brothers and sisters can be explained by Joseph's previous marriage. The more plausible scenario is that Mary and Joseph had several biological children together. For more on Jesus' family, see Richard Bauckham, "The Family of Jesus" in *Jesus among Friends and Enemies: A Historical and Literary Introduction to Jesus in the Gospels* (eds Chris Keith and Larry W. Hurtado) (Grand Rapids: Baker Academic, 2011), pp. 103–125.

7. Mark 6:3. Centuries later, various Christian writers speculated as to what the names of Jesus' sisters might be. These included Maria, Anna, Salome, Lysia, and Lydia.

8. To illustrate the exception to the rule, Mark gives no indication that he is aware of Jesus' father, Joseph. Jesus' mother, on the other hand, is mentioned by name multiple times.

9. Matt. 8:14; Mark 1:30; Luke 4:38.

10. 1 Cor. 9:5.

11. Clement interprets a line from the Letter to the Philippians as evidence that Paul was married (Phil. 4:3). According to Clement, "the only reason [Paul] did not take her around with him is that it would have been an inconvenience for his ministry" (*Stromateis*, 3.53). Clement also notes that Philip had daughters and he gave them in marriage.

12. *Proto-Gospel of James* 19:3–20:1.

13. Clement, *Stromateis*, 3.45.

14. Many Church Fathers believed that sin entered the world perpetually through procreation. Because sex was linked to childbirth, no human could be born without a nature of sin. Some believed that each woman who gave birth perpetuated Eve's sin and passed this sin nature on to her children. For more see DeConick, *Holy Misogyny*, esp. pp. 124–127.

15. Jennifer A. Glancy writes: "Mary is protected not only from sexual activity but also from the stain of menarche." Glancy sees this birth as the climax of a Gospel that is obsessed with purity. "Just as the [*Proto-Gospel of James*] implies that the Jerusalem temple is a sacred space that should not be polluted by womanly fluids, so the text implies that Mary's body is a sacred space. Mary's womb is Jesus' prenatal sanctuary. It should not be sullied by the usual sordid by-products of femininity." In Glancy, *Corporal Knowledge: Early Christian Bodies* (Oxford: Oxford University Press, 2010), pp. 108–109.

16. It is possible that all of these Salomes are fictional characters invented separately by early Christianity. Salome was a highly popular name during this period (perhaps made even more so by the beloved Shelamzion "Salome" Alexandra). I think the better solution is that these different historical fictions are based on a single historical figure.

17. *Gospel of Thomas* 61; some early Christians believed that the most high God was an undivided being, neither male nor female. Lesser deities were divided into male and female counterparts. This division was seen as the root problem that separated humanity from the enlightened mind of God. This saying in Thomas probably reflects the belief that being divided is problematic.

18. Luke 8:3.

19. Mark 15:40–41.

20. It should also be observed that Salome is appended to Jesus' legacy. In this way, we commemorate her within the frame of a male legacy. Admittedly, Jesus' historical gravitas trumps every figure to which it is associated in the stories related to his life and teachings.

21. Even modern scholars have attempted to find a man for Salome. Richard Bauckham makes an interesting argument that the Salome who affirms Mary's virginity is meant to be understood as the daughter of Joseph and the half-sister of Jesus. See Richard Bauckham, *Jude and the*

Relatives of Jesus in the Early Church (London: T & T Clark, 1990), p. 40. But the text does not indicate anything of the kind. I think it is far more likely that this portion of the *Proto-Gospel of James* has borrowed from an earlier virgin-birth narrative that is relatively independent from the birth narratives in Matthew and Luke but with specific knowledge of Mark. See George T. Zervos, "Seeking the Source for the Marian Myth: Have We Found the Missing Link?" in *Which Mary? The Marys of Early Christian Tradition* (ed. Stanley Jones) Society of Biblical Literature Symposium Series 19 (Atlanta: Society of Biblical Literature, 2002). The author of the birth narrative of *Proto-Gospel of James* seems to be aware that Salome is associated with the passion events that occur in Jerusalem.

22. Anne Lapidus Lerner, *Eternally Eve: Images of Eve in the Hebrew Bible* (Lebanon, NH: Brandeis University Press, 2007), pp. 167–168.

23. Ilan, *Silencing the Queen,* p. 20.

Chapter 3

1. DeConick, *Holy Misogyny,* p. xi.

2. *Gospel of Philip* 59; some argue that "kiss her often on the feet" is a better translation. The fragmentary nature of this passage will be discussed below.

3. *Gospel of Philip* 36.

4. *Gospel of Philip* 11–12.

5. Bart D. Ehrman, *Lost Christianities: The Battles for Scripture and the Faiths We Never Knew* (Oxford University Press, 2005), p. 122.

6. This group probably inherited a version of Christianity from a philosopher named Valentinus (born *c.* 100 C.E. and died *c.* 165 C.E.).

7. In this way, the Valentinians were similar to many versions of "gnostic" Christianity. The term gnosis literally means "knowledge." Gnostic Christians are generally described as Christians who sought salvation through special knowledge of heavenly matters. Another prominent feature of Gnostic thought was the view that the human spirit was trapped in an evil material world, created by a lesser god. Building from this mythology, Gnostic Christians believed that "salvation" included spiritual transcendence beyond the realm of the Hebrew God and into the presence of the "true God."

8. The *Gospel of Philip* makes a distinction between sex that is between spiritual equals and that which is not. Sex without spiritual solidarity is called adultery. It is possible that Philip's portrait of Jesus, representing perfectly transcendent humanity, included a model of union between male and female. If so, Mary might have been brought into this narrative because she was the most well-known female disciple of Jesus.
9. *Gospel of Philip* 99.
10. DeConick, *Misogyny*, p. 98.
11. Gen. 2:7.
12. John 20:22.
13. *Gospel of Thomas* 108.
14. *Gospel of Philip* 31.
15. Ehrman, *Lost Christianities*, p. 122.
16. Through personal correspondence, Mark Goodacre suggests that the text was originally "kissed her on the feet."
17. *Gospel of Thomas* 114. It is worth observing that Tal Ilan argues that one of the techniques to diminish and silence women during this period is to argue that the figure in question is really a man. In *Silencing the Queen*, pp. 20–25.
18. Gillian Clark, *Christianity and Roman Society: Key Themes in Ancient History* (Cambridge: Cambridge University Press, 2004), pp. 20–29.
19. This will be discussed further in chapters 8 and 9 of this book.
20. Paul Foster, *The Apocryphal Gospels: A Very Short Introduction* (Oxford: Oxford University Press, 2009), p. 48.

Chapter 4

1. Nikos Kazantzakis, *The Last Temptation of Christ* (trans. from Greek, 1953; New York: Simon & Schuster, 1960).
2. John P. Meier, *A Marginal Jew: Rethinking the Historical Jesus, Vol. 1* (New York: Doubleday, 1991), pp. 332–345.
3. Martin, *Sex and the Single Savior*, p. 96.
4. It might be helpful to remember that Mary was an extremely popular name during the time of Jesus. Scholar Tal Ilan has listed 247 names of women from 330 B.C.E.–200 C.E. Of these 247, 59 named women are called

"Mary". In *Lexicon of Jewish Names in Late Antiquity, Part I: Palestine 330 B.C.E.–200 C.E.; Texts and Studies in Ancient Judaism* 91 (Tübingen: Mohr Siebeck, 1989), p. 195. My thanks to Mark Goodacre for pointing me to this work.

5. *Homily* 33.

6. As one would expect, there were exceptions to this portrait. One of the more bizarre portraits of Jesus and Magdalene emerges from Catholic accusations of a group deemed heretical. In the early thirteenth century, a group called the "Cathars" were accused of teaching that Jesus was married to Mary Magdalene. In their view, Magdalene was one and the same with the "adulterous woman" of John 4:7–42. But it is extremely difficult to differentiate between what the Cathars taught and what they were accused of teaching. For example, they were accused of incest, bestiality, contraception, and so on. In other words, their theological opponents accused them of being anti-Catholic at every turn when it came to sexuality (and a host of other issues). On the contrary, the Cathars probably practiced sexual abstinence to a great extent. So we do not have an untainted window (via Roman Catholic propaganda and interrogation) into what this sect believed or taught. It is possible, however, that they believed that there were two Christs. The first Christ was heavenly and the second was earthly – the second being evil (or a pseudo-Christ). If the Cathars did indeed teach of this marriage, a further level of difficulty emerges in trying to determine which of the two Christs wed Magdalene. See Yuri Stoyanov, *The Other God: Dualist Religions from Antiquity to the Cathar Heresy* (New Haven: Yale University Press, 2000), pp. 278–280.

7. "Saint Mary Magdalene" in *The Golden Legend: Readings of the Saints* (Princeton: Princeton University Press, 2012), pp. 374–383, here 375.

8. Quoted from Alison Chapman, *Patrons and Patron Saints in Early Modern English Literature* (New York: Routledge, 2013), p. 123.

9. John Donne "To the Lady Magdalen Herbert: of St. Mary Magdalen (1607)" in *The Poems of John Donne*, vol. 1 (ed. Sir Herbert Grierson) (London: Oxford University Press, 1912), pp. 317–318.

10. Chapman, *Patrons and Patron Saints in Early Modern English Literature*, p. 124.

11. Cecil B. DeMille, *King of Kings* (Janus Films, 1927).

12. *The Last Temptation of Christ* (Universal Pictures, 1988).

13. Written by Paul Schrader; http://sfy.ru/?script=last_temptation_of_ christ_1988.

14. Darren J.N. Middleton, *Scandalizing Jesus?: Kazantzakis's* The Last Temptation of Christ *Fifty Years On* (London: Bloomsbury, 2005), pp. 148–149.

15. "Christmas Song" on *Remember Two Things* (RCA Records, 1997).

16. Stephen King, *The Dark Tower V: Wolves of the Calla* (New York: Simon & Schuster, 2003), p. 295.

17. Veronica Patterson, *Swan What Shores?* (New York: New York University Press, 2000), p. 23.

18. Dan Brown, *The Da Vinci Code* (reprint from 2003; New York: Anchor, 2009), pp. 319–320.

19. Compare Michael Baigent, Richard Leigh, Henry Lincoln, *The Holy Blood and the Holy Grail* (London: Jonathan Cape, 1982).

20. Karen King, provisional article at http://www.hds.harvard.edu/sites/hds. harvard.edu/files/attachments/faculty-research/research-projects/the-gospel-of-jesuss-wife/29865/King_JesusSaidToThem_draft_0920.pdf

21. Francis Watson, "The Gospel of Jesus' Wife: How a fake Gospel-Fragment was composed," p. 1; http://markgoodacre.org/Watson.pdf

22. Bernhard credits a conversation with Mark Goodacre that led to this observation: http://groups.yahoo.com/group/gthomas/message/ 10310; also see http://ntweblog.blogspot.co.uk/2012/10/jesus-wife-fragment-further-evidence-of.html

23. Except, of course, the phrase "my wife."

24. http://gospel-thomas.net/gtbypage_112702.pdf

25. http://www.nytimes.com/2012/09/19/us/historian-says-piece-of-papyrus-refers-to-jesus-wife.html

26. http://www.reuters.com/article/2012/09/19/us-religion-jesuswife-idUSBRE88I0520120919

Chapter 5

1. http://www.nytimes.com/2001/02/16/nyregion/affronted-by-nude-last-supper-giuliani-calls-for-decency-panel.html

2. However, see the insightful discussion of Sallman in Edward J. Blum and Paul Harvey, *The Color of Christ: The Son of God and the Saga of Race in America* (Chapel Hill: University of North Carolina Press, 2012), pp. 208–211.

See also Stephen Prothero, *American Jesus: How the Son of God Became a National Icon* (New York: Farrar, Straus and Giroux, 2004), pp. 116–123.

3. Richard S. Van Wagoner explains, "Polygamy, a criminal act under the 1833 Illinois Anti-bigamy Laws, was so unacceptable to monogamous nineteenth-century society that it could be introduced to the Church only in absolute secrecy." "Sarah Pratt: The Shaping of an Apostate" in *Dialogue: A Journal of Mormon Thought* 19.2 (1986), pp. 69–99, here p. 71.

4. John G. Turner, *Brigham Young: Pioneer, Prophet* (Cambridge, MA: Belknap Press of Harvard University, 2012), p. 91.

5. Brigham Young, "Gathering the Poor – Religion a Science" in *Journal of Discourses* 13 (1871), pp. 300–309, here p. 306.

6. Isa. 6:1.

7. Young, "Gathering the Poor," p. 306.

8. "Beneficial Effects of Polygamy: Remarks by President Brigham Young," *Journal of Discourses* 11 (1866), pp. 266–272, here p. 269.

9. Van Wagoner, "Sarah Pratt," p. 72.

10. Alongside many similar stories by excommunicated Mormons, William Law's testimony stands out: "Joseph is the liar and not she. That Smith admired and lusted after many men's wives and daughters, *is a fact*, but they could not help that. They or most of them considered his admiration an insult, and treated him with scorn. In return for this scorn, he generally managed to blacken their reputations – see the case of . . . Mrs. Pratt, a good, virtuous woman" in "Letter to the Salt Lake Tribune," 20 January 1887 (emphasis original).

11. In the early years of plural marriage in Nauvoo, Joseph Smith taught that the first wife must consent to her husband's taking of a second wife. When Sarah refused to give her consent, a caveat was amended to the original rule. The amendment stated that if a wife refused to consent, the husband may take an additional wife without consent.

12. Van Wagoner, "Sarah Pratt," p. 92.

13. *New York Herald*, 18 May 1877.

14. John 3:39.

15. Mark 2:20.

16. "Celestial Marriage" in *The Seer* vol. 1.11 (1853), pp. 169–176, here p. 170.

17. Jedediah M. Grant, "Uniformity" in *Journal of Discourses* vol. 1 (1854), pp. 341–349, here p. 345

18. Grant, "Uniformity," p. 346.

19. Origen's *Against Celsus* book 3, chapter 10; my thanks to Mark Wildish for pointing me to this parallel between this passage and Grant's claim.

20. It is also worth noting that Joseph Smith's polygamy and the dissent that it caused among his ranks played no small part in his eventual murder in 1844. After Smith's sexual advances toward the wives of Dr. Robert Foster and William Law, both men were excommunicated for their dissent. Foster and Law then established a publication called the *Nauvoo Expositor* for the purpose of exposing Smith's sexual misconduct and showing him to be a fallen prophet. This contributed greatly to the hostile climate that soon led to his death at the hands of an angry mob. Cf. Will Bagley, *Blood of the Prophets: Brigham Young and the Massacre at Mountain Meadows* (Oklahoma: University of Oklahoma Press, 2004), pp. 11–17. With this in mind, we find a parallel with Pratt's Jesus, who was persecuted for his practice of plural marriage and then martyred.

21. http://www.parade.com/celebrity/celebrity-parade/2010/elton-john-web-exclusive.html

22. http://abcnews.go.com/Entertainment/elton-john-jesus-super-intelligent-gay-man/story?id=9889098

23. Here I use the letters LGBT (as they have been used for the past decade) to refer to the lesbian, gay, bisexual, and transgender community. I should, however, acknowledge that some advocates include more letters: LGBTQIA. Here the Q can refer to "queer" (a derogatory term that has been rehabilitated in advocacy circles) or "questioning." I refer to "intersex" denoting anatomy that is not exclusively male or female. "A" can refer to "allies" of the community or "asexual."

24. http://www.huffingtonpost.com/2012/03/19/president-jimmy-carter-bible-book_n_1349570.html

25. I would categorize the recent comments by radio talk-show host Don Imus in the fourth category stated above: capitalist enterprise. His suggestion that Jesus was gay was most likely motivated by a desire to attract more attention to his program. Although one might argue that the motives for advertising dollars and social activism can and do overlap. http://www.huffingtonpost.com/2013/04/04/jesus-gay-don-imus-gospel-of-judas_n_3013535.html

26. It should be pointed out, however, that this notion was entertained as early as Christopher Marlowe (1564–1593) in literary circles.

27. Albert Baumgarton, "Smith, Morton (1915–91)" in *Dictionary of Biblical Interpretation: K–Z* (Nashville: Abingdon, 1999), p. 477.

28. William M. Calder III, "Morton Smith†," Gn. 64 (1992), pp. 382–383, here p. 382.

29. Stephen C. Carlson, *The Gospel Hoax: Morton Smith's Invention of* Secret Mark (Waco: Baylor University Press, 2005), p. 85.

30. The fact of the disappearance of this document is probably not the fault of Morton Smith. It does, however, contribute to the problems associated with testing the document and the mystery that hounds this story at every turn.

31. http://www.nysun.com/arts/unmasking-a-false-gospel/42197/

32. Eric Marcus, *Making Gay History: The Half Century Fight for Lesbian and Gay Equal Rights* (New York: HarperCollins, 2002), pp. 19–70.

33. Morton Smith, *Clement of Alexandria and a Secret Gospel of Mark* (Cambridge: Harvard University Press, 1973); Morton Smith, *The Secret Gospel: The Discovery and Interpretation of the Secret Gospel According to Mark* (New York: Harper & Row, 1973).

34. Morton Smith, "Psychiatric Practice and Christian Dogma" in *Journal of Pastoral Care* 3 (1949), pp. 12–20, here pp. 16–17.

35. Cf. Smith, "Psychiatric Practice," p. 12.

36. Smith, *The Secret Gospel*, p. 114; I credit Bart Ehrman for pointing out the particularly sexualized biases present in Smith's interpretation; see B.D. Ehrman, "Response to Charles Hedrick's Stalemate" in *JECS* 11 (2003), p. 157.

37. Baumgarton, "Smith, Morton (1915–91)," p. 477.

38. James H. Hunter, *The Mystery of Mar Saba* (Toronto: Evangelical Publishers, 1940).

39. Francis Watson, "Beyond Suspicion: On the Authorship of the Mar Saba Letter and the Secret Gospel of Mark," in *Journal of Theological Studies* 61.1 (2011), pp. 128–170, here pp. 169–170.

40. Dale Martin has recently considered (albeit cautiously) the possibility of a homosexual Jesus following Smith's lead: "Whatever one may think of Smith's hypothesis, one must admit it would solve some conundrums. The significance of the naked young man in the canonical Gospel of Mark is just one such problem. Perplexing parallels between the Gospels of Mark and John constitute another. And the Jesus of Smith's

reconstruction would go a long way toward explaining why Jesus may have never married" in *Sex and the Single Savior*, p. 96.

41. Carlson, *The Gospel Hoax*, p. 85.

Chapter 6

1. Michael Mills, Ph.D., as interviewed by Anastasia Toufexis for her *Time* article "The Right Chemistry," 2001; http://www.time.com/time/magazine/article/0,9171,161030,00.html

2. *Mad Men* is an AMC television series created and produced by Matthew Weiner. I quote here from an episode titled "Smoke Gets in Your Eyes" (season 1; episode 1) as quoted by Ada S. Jaarsma who comments: "Draper seems to get something right here about advertising's ability to create the desires of consumers . . . When he comments that 'guys like me' invented love to sell nylons, Draper is asserting an argument about our own susceptibility, as consumers, to the messages of brands' managers . . . Nylons, in Draper's example, are packaged under brand associations of 'romance' or 'falling in love.' In the specific case of nylons, the world's first synthetic stockings, DuPont's invention brought together modern science with domestic, feminine ease. Its successful market, however, did not employ the brand name DuPont since it reminded the public of 'chemistry.' Rather, the name of the product's material, 'nylon', became synonymous with the general category of 'stockings,' the branding so successful as to be rendered invisible . . . By branding nylons in terms of 'romantic love,' ad men like Don Draper are mobilizing other forces besides truth or logic that drive consumer choices – forces such as the longing for meaning and authenticity". Taken from "An Existential Look at *Mad Men*: Don Draper, Advertising, and the Promise of Happiness" in *Mad Men and Philosophy* (eds Rod Carveth and James B. South) (Hoboken, NJ: John Wiley & Sons, 2010), pp. 95–110; here pp. 96–98.

3. Tremper Longman III, *Song of Songs: The New International Commentary on the Old Testament* (Grand Rapids: Eerdmans, 2001), p. 59.

4. Persian influence on some portions of the biblical Song of Songs might suggest a much earlier date.

5. Here, "four limbs" can mean "arms and legs," but it might also be a metaphor for female genitalia.

6. Quoted from Joseph N. Bell, *Love Theory in Later Ḥanbalite Islam* (Albany: State University of New York Press, 1979), p. 134.

7. Unrequited love, while a popular theme in modern cultures, is not a common feature of ancient eroticism. Indeed, the *raison d'être* of most erotic poetry is to describe the physicality of sexual encounter and the emotions associated with this pursuit. Even if there are obstacles to achieving this, one normally expects those obstacles to be overcome.

8. Magda Bogin, *The Women Troubadors: An introduction to the women poets of 12th-century Provence and a collection of their poems* (New York: W.W. Norton & Company, Inc., 1980), p. 15.

9. Bogin, *The Women Troubadors*, p. 101.

10. See R. Howard Bloch, *Medieval Misogyny and the Invention of Western Romantic Love* (Chicago: University of Chicago Press, 1991), esp. pp. 113–142.

11. Marilyn Yalom, *How the French Invented Love: Nine Hundred Years of Passion and Romance* (New York: HarperCollins Publishers, 2012), p. 41.

12. C.S. Lewis, *The Allegory of Love* (1936, reprint, Oxford: Oxford University Press, 1970), p. 12.

13. Cultures of individualism can also value collective identity and well-being. Conversely, cultures of collectivism can also value individual desire, need, and achievement. The difference here is which concept of well-being is primary. I should also clarify that I do not intend to promote one cultural system as intrinsically better.

14. Ezra 9:12; compare Deut. 7:3.

15. Ezra 10:2–3.

16. Ezra 10:10–15.

17. Ezra 10:44.

18. Available for public viewing at: http://www.poetryfoundation.org/poem/173530

19. It should also be pointed out that this story serves as sacred scripture for many people. With this in mind, there have been numerous critiques and reinterpretations of this story to adapt it for many different audiences over the centuries. Stories like this one are not useful windows into the ideals of all of the groups that have claimed them as sacred.

20. In addition to the internal detractors of Ezra 9–10, it might be helpful to remember what the book of Jeremiah has to say on this subject: "Thus says the Lord of hosts, the God of Israel, to all the exiles whom

I have sent into exile from Jerusalem to Babylon: Build houses and live in them; plant gardens and eat what they produce. Take wives and have sons and daughters; take wives for your sons, and give your daughters in marriage, that they may bear sons and daughters; multiply there, and do not decrease. But seek the welfare of the city where I have sent you into exile, and pray to the Lord on its behalf, for in its welfare you will find your welfare" (Jer. 29:4–7).

21. Carol Meyers, "The Family in Early Israel" in *Families in Ancient Israel*, (eds D.S. Browning and E.S. Evison) (Louisville: Westminster John Knox, 1997), pp. 1–47, here p. 21.

22. A Roman philosopher of the first century C.E. named Gaius Musonius Rufus is a good counter-example to collectivism. He wrote: "Therefore those who contemplate marriage ought to have regard neither for family, whether either one be of highborn parents, nor for wealthy, whether on either side there be great possessions, nor for physical traits, whether one or the other have beauty. For neither wealth nor beauty nor high birth is effective in promoting partnership of interest or sympathy, nor again are they significant for producing children" in *Discourses* 13b. Notice that in this case, where Rufus argues against societal norms that would bespeak collectivism, the purposes of marriage are to promote partnership and to produce children. So even in cases of extreme "individualism" (if we may call it that), first-century notions of marriage were not romanticized, and look to promote family over individual desire/achievement. Further discussion about emerging "individualistic" nations of sexuality among urban eliles might consider the playful narratives of Greek erotic novels. For a recent discussion see Helen Morales, "The History of Sexualily" in *The Cambridge Companion to the Greek and Roman Novel* (ed. Tim Whitmarsh) (Cambridge: Cambridge University Press, 2008), pp. 39–55.

23. William E. Phipps, *Was Jesus Married?: The Distortion of Sexuality in the Christian Tradition* (Lantham, MD: University Press of America, 1986).

Chapter 7

1. Girls in modern, industrialized societies transition to puberty around the age of twelve. In pre-industrialized societies this age was probably closer to fifteen. The ancient, agrarian Mediterranean might have

NOTES

seen the age of puberty closer to fourteen. See J.H.J. Bancroft, *Human Sexuality and its Problems* (Edinburgh: Churchill Livingstone, 1989), p. 191. It is also important to note that maternal death during childbirth was a significant problem in the ancient world. As many as one in eight women died while giving birth in Roman-occupied territories. See T.G. Parkin, *Demography and Roman Society* (Baltimore: Johns Hopkins Press, 1992), pp. 103–105.

2. Luke 3:22–24.

3. Babylonian Talmud, Qiddushin 29b–30a. This text probably reflects an ideal and may not reflect standard practice.

4. Compare Meyers's assessment of early Israel in "The Family in Early Israel," p. 18, and Michael L. Satlow's assessment of the Bablyonian rabbis in *Jewish Marriage in Antiquity* (Princeton: Princeton University Press, 2001), p. 105; it is also worth noting that the Apostle Paul, who was a first-century Jew living in Judea, held ideas about marriage that were quite similar to these Babylonian rabbis. Paul seemed to value the ideal of celibacy but acknowledged that marriage was an acceptable institution. And like the ideas of the later Babylonian rabbis, Paul thought that marriage might provide an outlet for sexual desire. So we see that sometimes these rabbinic ideas stem from the seeds of a much earlier time period.

5. For example, these rabbis discuss betrothal, but the practice of "betrothal" may not have been commonly practiced before the second century. See Hayim Lapin, *Rabbis as Romans: The Rabbinic Movement in Palestine, 100–400 CE* (Oxford: Oxford University Press, 2012), pp. 133–134.

6. Tim Parkin and Arthur Pomeroy, *Roman Social History: A Sourcebook* (New York: Routledge, 2007), pp. 46–58.

7. Relatedly, Satlow writes that the Mishnah (m. Yeb. 10.18; m. Nid. 5.4) establishes the minimum "legal age of marriage at nine for a male and three for a female." He is careful to qualify that "the minimum legal age of marriage says nothing about what people actually did, and only slightly more about their ideals" (*Jewish Marriage in Antiquity,* p. 307).

8. Meyers, "The Family in Early Israel," p. 21.

9. 1QSa 1:9–11.

10. Lynn Cohick, *Women in the World of the Earliest Christians: Illuminating Ancient Ways of Life* (Grand Rapids: Baker Academic, 2009), p. 119; compare the more focused study of Adiel Schremer, "Men's Age at Marriage in Jewish Palestine of the Hellenistic and Roman Periods" in *Zion* 61 (1996): pp. 45–66.

11. Satlow suggests that Babatha's first husband (Jesus, son of Jesus) was likely a child in 110 C.E. when he received a legal transfer of his father's estate. If so, he was likely in his early twenties when he married Babatha (*Jewish Marriage in Antiquity*, p. 97).

12. N. Lewis and M. Reinhold, *Roman Civilization, Vol. 2* (New York: Harper & Row, 1955), pp. 48–52.

13. These laws included penalties and incentives for the transfer inheritance. This demonstrates how closely tied were marriage, family, and economics in this context. In the next chapter, I will revisit this idea in my discussion of "civic masculinity."

14. Yebam, 10.9g.

15. Satlow, *Jewish Marriage in Antiquity*, p. 104.

16. John 8:41.

17. Did the accounts of Jesus' divinely conceived birth cause some to think that he was really illegitimate? Or did the rumors of Jesus' illegitimacy inspire the stories about Jesus' birth? I would guess that these two interpretations of Jesus are related in some way, but I cannot say how.

18. Luke 2:40.

Chapter 8

1. Susan E. Haddox, "Favoured Sons and Subordinate Masculinities" in *Men and Masculinity in the Hebrew Bible and Beyond: Bible in the Modern World* 33 (ed. Ovidiu Creangă) (Sheffield: Sheffield Phoenix, 2010), pp. 2–19, here pp. 6–7; Haddox draws from David J.A. Clines, *Interested Parties: The Ideology of Writers and Readers of the Hebrew Bible: Journal for the Study of the Old Testament Supplement Series* 205 (Sheffield: Sheffield Academic Press, 1995), pp. 212–241.

2. The important distinction here is between "hegemonic" and "subordinate" masculinities. These four criteria are generally associated with varieties of hegemonic masculinity.

3. See Colleen Conway, *Behold the Man: Jesus and Greco-Roman Masculinity* (Oxford: Oxford University Press, 2008).

4. Exod. 20:12.

5. Jerome H. Neyrey, "Jesus, Gender, and the Gospel of Matthew," in *New Testament Masculinities; Semeia* 45 (Atlanta: Society of Biblical Literature, 2003), pp. 43–66, here p. 48.

6. Consider the Pauline instruction for men who aspire to leadership in the Church: "He must manage his own household well, keeping his children submissive and respectful in every way; for if a man does not know how to manage his own household, how can he care for God's church?" (1 Tim. 3:4–5).

7. Neyrey, "Jesus, Gender, and the Gospel of Matthew," p. 44.

8. Compare Lilian Portefaix, "Good Citizenship in the Household of God: Women's Positions in the Pastorals Reconsidered in the Light of Roman Rule" in *A Feminist Companion to the Deutero-Pauline Epistles* (eds Amy-Jill Levine with Marianne Blickenstaff) (Cleveland: The Pilgrim Press, 2003), pp. 147–158, here p. 154.

9. *Annals* 3.25.

10. Matt. 19:12

11. Matt. 19:11.

12. Dale C. Allison Jr. writes: "These words are sometimes construed, in their Matthean context, as recommending that those who have separated from a spouse should not remarry. The more likely interpretation is that Mt 19:10–12 is about life long celibacy." In Dale C. Allison, *Jesus of Nazareth: Millenarian Prophet* (Minneapolis: Fortress, 1998), p. 175.

13. Given that concerns about celibacy were heating up during this period in the larger Roman Empire, it is not surprising to see Jesus discussing the topic with his disciples. In this case, Jesus might be taking a stance against Roman law. For more on this possibility, see Halvor Moxnes, *Putting Jesus in His Place: A Radical Vision of Household and Kingdom* (Westminster John Knox, 2003).

14. Deut. 23:1. Compare Mark K. George, "Masculinity and Its Regimentation in Deuteronomy," in *Men and Masculinity in the Hebrew Bible and Beyond*, pp. 64–82, here p. 77.

15. Luke 18:28; compare Matt. 19:27.

16. If we accept (a) that many of Jesus' disciples had left their wives behind to

follow him and (b) that many women were included in Jesus' following, could this provide the context for Jesus' strange teaching about divorce? Jesus seems to take a more rigid stance on divorce than any of his Jewish contemporaries. Jesus seems to have strongly discouraged men from divorcing their wives and forbade men and women from remarrying (Matt. 5:31–32; 19:1–12; Mark 10:1–12; Luke 16:18; 1 Cor. 7:10–11). Given Jesus' praise of eunuchs, and those who have left their wives and houses behind, it comes as no surprise to hear him discourage remarriage. Could it be that he was discouraging his male disciples (who had left wives behind) from marrying the female followers with whom they traveled? In other words, perhaps Jesus is saying, "So you've left your wives behind to follow me; great! But don't use that as justification for divorcing your wives to marry one of your traveling companions!" This possible reading would also help to explain this saying, "You have heard that it was said, 'You shall not commit adultery.' But I say to you that everyone who looks at a woman [or wife] with lust has already committed adultery with her in his heart" (Matt. 5:27–28). It is also worth noting that a legally terminated marriage often had dire consequences for the woman, who was cut off from her family (and therefore economic) network.

17. Matt. 10:34–36.

18. Luke 14:26; compare *Gospel of Thomas* 55.

19. Stephen Moore and Janice Capel Anderson write: "The downplaying of literal familial relationships, and the corresponding elevation of spiritual or fictive kinship, thereby clearing the way for alternative models of masculinity, is followed through the remainder of [Matthew's] Gospel – although not without ambivalence." ("Matthew and Masculinity" in *New Testament Masculinities; Semeia* 45 (eds Stephen Moore and Janice Capel Anderson) (Atlanta: Society of Biblical Literature, 2003), pp. 67–92, here p. 75.

20. Matt. 12:46–50.

21. Another example: "No servant can serve two masters; for either he will hate the one and love the other, or he will be devoted to the one and despise the other. You cannot serve God and mammon" (Luke 16:13; compare *Gospel of Thomas* 47).

22. For more on Jesus' relationship with his mother, see Anthony Le Donne,

Historical Jesus: What Can We Know and How Can We Know It? (Grand Rapids: Eerdmans, 2010), pp. 42–52.

23. Luke 11:27–28; compare also *Gospel of Thomas* 79. Joel B. Green asks rhetorically: "Had not Jesus redefined family when he said, 'My mother and my brothers are those who hear the word of God and do it' (Luke 8:21 [cf. 3:7–14])?" in *Practicing Theological Interpretation: Engaging Biblical Texts for Faith and Formation* (Grand Rapids: Baker Academic, 2011), p. 62.

24. Compare *Gospel of Thomas* 86.

25. Matt. 8:19–22.

26. E.P. Sanders suggested that this was one of the few sayings indicating that Jesus acted contrary to Jewish legal instruction, in *Jesus and Judaism* (Minneapolis: Fortress Press, 1985), pp. 252–255, p. 267.

27. Compare also the story of Jesus and the rich young man who wishes to follow Jesus (Mark 10:17–27). Jesus commands him to sell all of his possessions and give the money to the poor. The young man decides not to follow Jesus. Jesus then reflects: "How hard it will be for those who have wealth to enter the kingdom of God!"

28. Matt. 6:25. Dale C. Allison Jr. suggests: "Jesus' free attitude toward property may also have had an element of proleptic eschatology. For Genesis 3 makes it plain that, before they succumbed to temptation, Adam and Eve did not have to toil in the cursed ground and eat bread by the sweat of their faces . . . Nor did they need clothing. Business and money, then, were not part of their world. One wonders whether Jesus' call to live without anxiety for food and clothing . . . originally harked back to the primeval state" (*Millenarian Prophet,* p. 210).

Chapter 9

1. Co-authored with Martin Dugard, *Killing Jesus: A History* (New York: Henry Holt and Co., 2013).

2. Matt. 16:28.

3. Martin, *Sex and the Single Savior,* p. 106.

4. Mark 18:20.

5. Adela Yarbro Collins, *Mark: A Commentary; Hermeneia: A Critical and Historical Commentary on the Bible* (Minneapolis: Fortress, 2007), p. 199.

6. For example, Isa. 54:4–6; 61:10; Jer. 2:2; Ezek. 16:8–16. It is worth noting, however, that Michael Satlow suggests that the metaphor of husband and wife used to relate God and Israel was not popular in Jewish thought until much later. He argues that Judaism exploited the metaphor long after Christianity had applied it to Christ and the Church. So Christianity adapted the metaphor from Judaism and then Judaism adapted it back. Of course, this sort of "sharing" happens more often than we might think between sibling religions (*Jewish Marriage in Antiquity,* pp. 42–67).

7. For example, Deut. 28:4–6; Isa. 25:6; Joel 2:19.

8. John 2:1–11.

9. Marianne Blickenstaff argues that Matthew's Gospel moves in this direction: "I propose that the Matthean Jesus community should be defined not only as a new family composed of the child of God the Father, but also as [children] who anticipate the eschatological wedding banquet, even as they celebrate Jesus' presence as a bridegroom among them" (*"While the Bridegroom is with them": Marriage, Family, Gender and Violence in the Gospel of Matthew* (Edinburgh: T & T Clark, 2005), p. 112.

10 Rev. 19:7.

11. Most scholars date the book of Revelation to 95 C.E. Some place its authorship before 70 C.E.

12. Song of Songs 5:2.

13. Rev. 3:20.

14. Song of Songs 5:3–6 (New American Standard).

15. I agree with David Aune that the symbolism here is polyvalent. That is to say that John has drawn from several overlapping cultural images to build this scene. Aune also points to a line from *Hymn to Apollo* 3: "It must be that Phoebus, with beautiful foot, kicks at the door." David Aune, *Revelation,* Word Biblical Commentary 52a (Waco: Word Publishers, 1997), pp. 250–260; "foot" was a well-known euphemism for the penis in the ancient Mediterranean.

16. Compare Rev. 19:8. I translate δικαιώματα as "acts of right-relationship."

17. Rev. 19:7–8.

18. Rev. 19:9.

19. Song of Songs 2:4.

20. For more on idealized women in civic margins, see Kate Cooper, *The Virgin and the Bride: Idealized Womanhood in Late Antiquity* (Cambridge: Harvard University Press, 1996).

21. For an idealized example: Acts 2:44–46: "And all who believed were together and had all things in common, and they sold their possessions and goods and distributed them to all, as any had need. And day by day, attending the temple together and breaking bread in their homes, they partook of food with glad and generous hearts." For more on this portrait of early Christianity see Anthony Le Donne, "The Improper Temple Offerings of Ananias and Sapphira," *New Testament Studies* 59 (2013), pp. 1–19. For an indication of a concrete reality fraught with difficulty, see 2 Cor. 8.

22. 2 Cor. 8:14.

23. 2 Cor. 11:2.

24. Irenaeus, *Against Heresies*, 1.28.

25. Clement, *Stromateis* 3.49.

26. Clement, *Stromateis* 3.74.

27. Elaine H. Pagels, "Adam and Eve, Christ and the Church: A Survey of Second Century Controversies concerning Marriage" in *The New Testament and Gnosis: Essays in Honour of Robert McL. Wilson* (eds Alastair Logan and Alexander J.M. Wedderburn) (London: T & T Clark, 1983), pp. 146–175, here pp. 151–152.

28. Anonymous, *The Lady Poverty: A XIII Century Allegory* (trans. Montgomery Carmichael) (London: John Murray, 1901).

29. The belief that Jesus went without shoes might stem from Matt. 10:9–10: "Take no gold, nor silver, nor copper in your belts, no bag for your journey, nor two tunics, nor sandals, nor a staff; for the laborer deserves his food."

30. Building from the Benedictine rule that forbids private ownership of property, Francis's order established a vow of poverty. In practice, however, Francis took poverty to an extreme uncommon among Benedictine monks.

Chapter 10

1. Marilyn Yalom, *History of the Breast* (New York: Ballantine Books, 1998), p. 5.

2. *Proto-Gospel of James* 19.

3. Luke 11:27–28.

4. *Gospel of Thomas* 79.

5. Compare Yalom, *History of the Breast*, pp. 27–28. A variety of practices were discussed in the ancient world relating to wet nurses and emergency use of animal milk, but the common practice of breastfeeding was not questioned.

6. Mosseri 7.68.A; adapted from Satlow, *Jewish Marriage in Antiquity*, p. 3.

7. Gen. 1:28.

8. Satlow, *Jewish Marriage in Antiquity*, p. 112.

9. As discussed, puberty was probably entered between the ages of fourteen and twenty for boys, depending on nourishment.

10. *Mishnah, Aboth* 5.21.

11. Examples of symbolic ages are common in the Hebrew Bible, but to point to an example from Jesus' time, consider this instruction from the Dead Sea Scrolls: "The men of the army shall be from forty to fifty years old. The commissioners of the camps shall be from fifty to sixty years old. The officers shall also be from forty to fifty years old" (*War Scroll* 7.1–2). Taken literally, this instruction for battle is absurd. Most men would have been dead or declining by fifty; able-bodied soldiers would have been much younger than forty.

12. Luke 3:23.

13. John P. Meier lists a handful of examples including Greek Philosopher Epictetus (55–35 B.C.E.) and philosopher and wonderworker Apollonius of Tyana (*Marginal Jew I*, pp. 342, 367).

14. Luke 3:7–8; compare Matt. 3:7–9.

15. To Semitic ears (either Hebrew or Aramaic) there is a wordplay happening here. The phrase "sons" is either alliterative or homophonic to the word for "stones." One wonders if John the Baptist's Jewish audience would have heard this saying as humorous.

16. *Gospel of Thomas* 79.

17. Luke 14:26; compare Matt. 10:35–36.

18. Matt. 8:21–22.

19. Luke 2:48–49; the narrator attempts to smooth over this obvious tension between Jesus and his parents in the verses that follow.

20. Mark 3:32–34.

21. John 2:4; the phrase "what have you to do with me?" sounds even more hostile in the Greek and Aramaic. This idiom is used by "demon-possessed" men to violently rebuke Jesus in Mark 1:24 and 5:7. It is the hostile protest of someone who is about to be tormented or forcibly made to do something against his or her will.

22. Mark 3:21.

23. Luke 11:27; *Gospel of Thomas* 79.

24. Luke 11:28.

25. It is also important to remember the portrait of Jesus' crucifixion in the Gospel of John: "When Jesus saw his mother, and the disciple whom he loved standing near, he said to his mother, 'Woman, behold, your son!' Then he said to the disciple, 'Behold, your mother!' And from that hour the disciple took her to his own home" (John 19:26–27). In this portrait, Jesus reinforces his followers as a metaphorical family. The beloved disciple and the mother of Jesus were bound together, but not biologically bound.

26. Hosea 9:11, 14.

27. Mark 12:25; compare Matt. 22:30; Luke 20:35; Jewish lore gives the general impression that angels are male.

28. Luke 20:34–36.

29. Matt. 19:12

30. Luke 18:28; compare Matt. 19:27.

Afterword

1. Nikos Kazantzakis, "Prologue" in *The Last Temptation of Christ* (New York: Simon and Schuster, 1998), pp. 1–3 (emphasis mine).

2. Kazantzakis, *The Last Temptation of Christ*, p. 3.

3. Nikos Kazantzakis, "Author's Introduction" in *Report to Greco* (New York: Simon and Schuster, 1965), p. 15.

BIBLIOGRAPHY

Allison Jr., Dale C. *Jesus of Nazareth: Millenarian Prophet*. Minneapolis: Fortress, 1998.

Anonymous, *The Lady Poverty: A XIII Century Allegory*. Translated by Montgomery Carmichael. London: John Murray, 1901.

Atkinson, Kenneth. *Queen Salome: Jerusalem's Warrior Monarch of the First Century B.C.E.* Jefferson: Mcfarland, 2012.

Aune, David. *Revelation; Word Biblical Commentary* 52a. Waco: Word Publishers, 1997.

Bagley, Will. *Blood of the Prophets: Brigham Young and the Massacre at Mountain Meadows*. Oklahoma: University of Oklahoma Press, 2004.

Baigent, Michael, Richard Leigh, Henry Lincoln. *The Holy Blood and the Holy Grail*. London: Jonathan Cape, 1982.

Bancroft, J.H.J. *Human Sexuality And Its Problems*. Edinburgh: Churchhill Livingstone, 1989.

Bauckham, Richard. *Jude and the Relatives of Jesus in the Early Church*. London: T & T Clark, 1990.

____ "The Family of Jesus." Pages 103–125 in *Jesus Among Friends and Enemies: A Historical and Literary Introduction to Jesus in the Gospels*. Edited by Chris Keith and Larry Hurtado. Grand Rapids: Baker Academic Press, 2011.

Baumgarton, Albert. "Smith, Morton (1915–91)," Page 477 in *Dictionary of Biblical Interpretation: K-Z*. Nashville: Abingdon, 1999.

Bell, Joseph N. *Love Theory in Later Hanbalite Islam*. Albany: State University of New York Press, 1979.

Blenkinsopp, Joseph. *Ezra-Nehemiah: A Commentary. The Old Testament Library.* Philadelphia: The Westminster Press, 1988.

Blickenstaff, Marianne. *'While the Bridegroom is with them': Marriage, Family, Gender and Violence in the Gospel of Matthew.* London: T&T Clark, 2005.

Bloch, R. Howard. *Medieval Misogyny and the Invention of Western Romantic Love.* Chicago: University of Chicago Press, 1991.

Blum, Edward J. and Paul Harvey. *The Color of Christ: The Son of God and the Saga of Race in America.* Chapel Hill: University of North Carolina Press, 2012.

Bockmuehl, Markus. *Simon Peter in Scripture and Memory: The New Testament Apostle in the Early Church.* Grand Rapids: Baker Academic, 2012.

Boer, Esther A. de, and John Bowden. *The Mary Magdalene Cover-Up: The Sources Behind the Myth.* London: T & T Clark, 2006.

Bogin, Magda. *The Women Troubadors: An Introduction to the Women Poets of the 12th-century Provence and a Collective of Their Poems.* New York: W.W. Norton & Company, Inc., 1980.

Brakke, David. *The Gnostics: Myth, Ritual, and Diversity in Early Christianity.* Cambridge: Harvard University Press, 2010.

Brown, Dan. *The Da Vinci Code.* New York: Anchor, 2009.

Brown, Peter. *The Body and Society: Men, Women, and Sexual Renunciation in Early Christianity.* New York: Columbia University Press, 1988.

Burke, Tony (Editor). *Ancient Gospel or Modern Forgery?* The Secret Gospel of Mark *in Debate: Proceedings from the 2011 York University Christian Apocrypha Symposium.* Eugene: Wipf & Stock, 2013.

Calder III, William M. "Morton Smith†," Gn. 64 (1992), 382–83, here 382.

Carlson, Stephen C. *The Gospel Hoax: Morton Smith's Invention of Secret Mark.* Waco: Baylor University Press, 2005.

Chapman, Alison. *Patrons and Patron Saints in Early Modern English Literature.* New York: Routledge, 2013.

Childs, Hal. *The Myth of the Historical Jesus and the Evolution of Consciousness. Society of Biblical Literature Dissertation Series* 179. Atlanta: Society of Biblical Literature, 2000.

Clark, Elizabeth. *St. Augustine on Marriage and Sexuality: Selections from the Fathers of the Church.* Washington D.C.: Catholic University of America Press, 1996.

Clark, Gillian. *Christianity and Roman Society: Key Themes in Ancient History.* Cambridge: Cambridge University Press, 2004.

Clines, David J.A. *Interested Parties: The Ideology of Writers and Readers of the Hebrew Bible; Journal for the Study of the Old Testament Supplement Series 205; Gender, Culture, Theory 1.* Sheffield: Sheffield Academic Press, 1995.

Cohick, Lynn. *Women in the World of the Earliest Christians: Illuminating Ancient Ways of Life.* Grand Rapids: Baker Academic, 2009.

Collins, Adela Yarbro. *Mark: A Commentary; Hermeneia: A Critical and Historical Commentary on the Bible.* Minneapolis: Fortress, 2007.

Conway, Colleen. *Behold the Man: Jesus and Greco-Roman Masculinity.* Oxford: Oxford University Press, 2008.

Cooper, Kate. *The Virgin and the Bride: Idealized Womanhood in Late Antiquity.* Cambridge: Harvard University Press, 1996.

Davies, Douglas J. *An Introduction to Mormonism.* Cambridge: Cambridge University Press, 2003.

DeConick, April D. *The Original Gospel of Thomas in Translation: With a Commentary and New English Translation of the Complete Gospel: Library of New Testament Studies.* London: T & T Clark, 2007.

___ *Holy Misogyny: Why the Sex and Gender Conflicts in the Early Church Still Matter.* New York: Continuum Press, 2011.

Donne, John. *The Poems of John Donne.* Volume 1. Edited by Sir Herbert Grierson. Oxford: Clarendon Press, 1912.

Dunn, James D. G. *Christian Liberty: A New Testament Perspective: The Didsbury Lectures.* Carlisle: Paternoster Press, 1993.

Ehrman, Bart D. "Response to Charles Hedrick's Stalemate," *JECS* 11 (2003): 155–63.

___ *Lost Christianities: The Battles for Scripture and the Faiths We Never Knew.* Oxford University Press, 2005.

___ *Truth and Fiction in The Da Vinci Code: A Historian Reveals What We Really Know about Jesus, Mary Magdalene, and Constantine.* Oxford: Oxford University Press, 2004.

Falsani, Cathleen. *The Dude Abides: The Gospel According to the Coen Brothers.* Grand Rapids: Zondervan, 2009.

Foster, Paul. *The Apocryphal Gospels: A Very Short Introduction.* Oxford: Oxford University Press, 2009.

Francis, James. *Subversive Virtue: Asceticism and Authority in the Second-Century Pagan World.* University Park: Pennsylvania State University Press, 1994.

George, Mark K. "Masculinity and Its Regimentation in Deuteronomy." Pages 64–82 in *Men and Masculinity in the Hebrew Bible and Beyond; Bible in the Modern World* 33. Edited by Ovidiu Creangă. Sheffield: Sheffield Phoenix, 2010.

Glancy, Jennifer A. *Corporal Knowledge: Early Christian Bodies.* Oxford: Oxford University Press, 2010.

Grant, Jedediah M. "Uniformity" *Journal of Discourses* 1 (1854): 341–49.

Green, Joel B. *Practicing Theological Interpretation: Engaging Biblical Texts for Faith and Formation.* Grand Rapids: Baker Academic, 2011.

Haddox, Susan E. "Favoured Sons and Subordinate Masculinities" Pages 2–19 in *Men and Masculinity in the Hebrew Bible and Beyond; Bible in the Modern World* 33. Edited by Ovidiu Creangă. Sheffield: Sheffield Phoenix, 2010.

Hanson, K. C. and Douglas E. Oakman. *Palestine in the Time of Jesus: Social Structures and Social Conflicts.* Minneapolis: Fortress Press, 2008.

Hunter, James H. *The Mystery of Mar Saba.* Toronto: Evangelical Publishers, 1940.

Ilan, Tal. *Lexicon of Jewish Names in Late Antiquity,Part I: Palestine 330 BCE-200 CE; Texts and Studies in Ancient Judaism* 91. Tübingen: Mohr Siebeck, 1989.

____ *Silencing the Queen: The Literary Histories of Shelamzion and Other Jewish Women, Texte und Studien zum Antiken Judentum* 115. Tübingen: Mohr Siebeck, 2006.

Jaarsma, Ada S. "An Existential Look at *Mad Men:* Don Draper, Advertising, and the Promise of Happiness" Pages 95–110 in *Mad Men and Philosophy.* Edited by Rod Carveth and James B. South. Hoboken: John Wiley & Sons, 2010.

Jacobs, Sandra. "Divine Virility in Priestly Representation: Its Memory and Consummation in Rabbinic Midrash." Pages 146–70 in *Men and Masculinity in the Hebrew Bible and Beyond; Bible in the Modern World* 33. Edited by Ovidiu Creangă. Sheffield: Sheffield Phoenix, 2010.

Kazantzakis, Nikos. *The Last Temptation of Christ.* New York: Simon Schuster, 1960.

___ "Author's Introduction." Pages 14–15 in *Report to Greco*. New York: Simon and Schuster, 1965.

___ "Prologue." Pages 1–3 in *The Last Temptation of Christ*. New York: Simon and Schuster, 1998.

Keith, Chris. *Jesus' Literacy: Scribal Culture and the Teacher from Galilee*. London: Bloomsbury, 2011.

King, Karen L. *The Gospel of Mary of Magdala: Jesus and the First Woman Apostle*. Santa Rosa: Poleridge Press, 2003.

King, Stephen. *The Dark Tower V: Wolves of the Calla*. New York: Simon & Schuster, 2003.

Kuefler, Matthew. *The Manly Eunuch: Masculinity, Gender Ambiguity, and Christian Ideology in Late Antiquity*. Chicago: The University of Chicago Press, 2001.

Lapin, Hayim. *Rabbis as Romans: The Rabbinic Movement in Palestine, 100–400 CE*. Oxford: Oxford University Press, 2012.

Le Donne, Anthony. *Historical Jesus: What Can We Know and How Can We Know It?* Grand Rapids: Eerdmans, 2010.

___ "The Improper Temple Offerings of Ananias and Sapphira," *New Testament Studies* 59 (2013): 1–19.

Lerner, Anne Lapidus. *Eternally Eve: Images of Eve in the Hebrew Bible*. Lebanon, NH: Brandeis University Press, 2007.

Levine, Amy-Jill with Maria Mayo Robbins. *A Feminist Companion to the New Testament Apocrypha: Feminist Companion to the New Testament and Early Christian Writings*. Cleveland: Pilgrim Press, 2006.

Lewis, C.S. *The Allegory of Love*. Oxford: Oxford University Press, 1970.

Lewis, Naphtali and Meyer Reinhold. *Roman Civilization. Volume 2*. New York: Harper & Row, 1955.

Longman III, Tremper. *Song of Songs. The New International Commentary on the Old Testament*. Grand Rapids: Eerdmans, 2001.

Marcus, Eric. *Making Gay History: The Half Century Fight for Lesbian and Gay Equal Rights*. New York: HarperCollins, 2002.

Martin, Dale B. *Sex and the Single Savior: Gender and Sexuality in Biblical Interpretation*. Louisville: Westminster John Knox Press, 2006.

Matera II, Frank J. *Corinthians: A Commentary: New Testament Library*. Louisville: Westminster/John Knox, 2003.

Meier, John P. *A Marginal Jew: Rethinking the Historical Jesus. Volume 1*. New York: Doubleday, 1991.

Meyers, Carol. "The Family in Early Israel." Pages 1–47 in *Families in Ancient Israel*. Edited by D.S. Browning and E.S. Evison. Louisville: Westminster John Knox, 1997.

Middleton, Darren J. N. *Scandalizing Jesus?: Kazantzakis's The Last Temptation of Christ Fifty Years On*. London: Bloomsbury, 2005.

Moore, Stephen and Janice Capel Anderson. "Matthew and Masculinity" Pages 67–92 in *New Testament Masculinities; Semeia 45*. Atlanta: Society of Biblical Literature, 2003.

Morales, Helen. "The History of Sexuality." Pages 39–55 in *The Cambridge Companion to the Greek and Roman Novel*. Edited by Tim Whitmarsh. Cambridge: Cambridge University Press, 2008.

Morton, Smith, "Psychiatric Practice and Christian Dogma" in *Journal of Pastoral Care* 3 (1949): 12–20.

_____ *Clement of Alexandria and a Secret Gospel of Mark*. Cambridge: Harvard University Press, 1973.

_____ *The Secret Gospel: The Discovery and Interpretation of the Secret Gospel According to Mark*. New York: Harper & Row, 1973.

Neyrey, Jerome H. "Jesus, Gender, and the Gospel of Matthew," Pages 43–66 in *New Testament Masculinities; Semeia 45*. Atlanta: Society of Biblical Literature, 2003.

O'Reilly, Bill, with Martin Dugard. *Killing Jesus: A History*. New York: Henry Holt and Co., 2013.

Pagels, Elaine H. "Adam and Eve, Christ and the Church: a Survey of Second Century Controversies concerning Marriage." Pages 146–75 in *The New Testament and Gnosis: Essays in honour of Robert McL. Wilson*. Edited by Alastair Logan, Alexander J. M. Wedderburn. London: T & T Clark, 1983.

Parkin, Tim and Arthur Pomeroy. *Roman Social History: A Sourcebook*. New York: Routledge, 2007.

Parkin, T.G. *Demography and Roman Society*. Baltimore: Johns Hopkins Press, 1992.

Patterson, Veronica. *Swan What Shores?* New York: New York Univ. Press, 2000.

Portefaix, Lilian. "Good Citizenship in the Household of God: Women's Positions in the Pastorals Reconsidered in the Light of Roman Rule." Pages 147–158 in *A Feminist Companion to the Deutero-Pauline Epistles*. Edited by Amy-Jill Levine with Marianne Blickenstaff. Cleveland: The Pilgrim Press, 2003.

Prothero, Stephen. *American Jesus: How the Son of God Became a National Icon*. New York: Farrar, Straus and Giroux, 2004.

Pruss, Alexander R. *One Body: An Essay in Christian Sexual Ethics*; ND Studies in Ethics and Culture. Notre Dame, IN: University of Notre Dame Press, 2012.

Roof, Judith. "Living the James Bond Lifestyle." Pages 71–86 in *Ian Fleming and James Bond: The Cultural Politics of 007*. Edited by Edward P. Comentale, Stephen Watt, and Skip Willman. Bloomington: Indiana University Press, 2005.

Sanders, E. P. *Jesus and Judaism*. Minneapolis: Fortress Press, 1985.

Satlow, Michael L. *Jewish Marriage in Antiquity*. Princeton: Princeton University Press, 2001.

Schaberg, Jane, with Melanie Johnson-Debaufre. *Mary Magdalene Understood*. New York: Continuum, 2006.

Schremer, Adiel. "Men's Age at Marriage in Jewish Palestine of the Hellenistic and Roman Periods," *Zion* 61 (1996): 45–66.

Skinner, Christopher W. *What Are They Saying About the Gospel of Thomas?* Mahwah, NJ: Paulist Press, 2012.

Stoyanov, Yuri. *The Other God: Dualist Religions from Antiquity to the Cathar Heresy*. New Haven: Yale University Press, 2000.

Tan, Yak-Hwee. "The Question of Social Location and Postcolonial Feminist Hermeneutics of Liberation." Pages 171–78 in *Feminist Interpretation of The Bible*. Edited by Silvia Schroer and Sophia Bietenhard. London: Sheffield Academic Press, 2003.

Thompson, Augustine. *Francis of Assisi: A New Biography*. Ithaca, NY: Cornell University Press, 2012.

Triandis, Harry C. *Individualism And Collectivism. New Directions in Social Psychology*. Boulder: Westview Press, 1995.

Turner, John G. *Brigham Young: Pioneer, Prophet*. Cambridge: Belknap Press of Harvard University, 2012.

Valantasis, Richard. *The Gospel of Thomas: New Testament Readings.* New York: Routledge, 1997.

Van Wagoner, Richard S. "Sarah Pratt: The Shaping of an Apostate." *Dialogue: A Journal of Mormon Thought* 19.2 (1986): 69–99.

VanderKam, James. *The Dead Sea Scrolls Today.* Revised Edition. Grand Rapids: Eerdmans, 2010.

Voragine, Jacobus De. "Saint Mary Magdalene." Pages 374–83 in *The Golden Legend: Readings of the Saints.* Princeton: Princeton University Press, 2012.

Waley, Arthur. *Translations from the Chinese.* New York: Alfred A. Knoph, 1941.

Walzer, Richard. *Galen on Jews and Christians.* London: Oxford University, 1949.

Watson, Francis. "Beyond Suspicion: on the Authorship of the Mar Saba Letter and the Secret Gospel of Mark," *Journal of Theological Studies* 61.1 (2011): 128–170.

Watterson, Bill. *Homicidal Psycho Jungle Cat: A Calvin and Hobbes Collection.* Kansas City, Mo.: Andrews McMeel Publishing, 1994.

Wimbush, Vincent L. and Richard Valantasis (Editors). *Asceticism.* Oxford: Oxford University Press, 1998.

Yalom, Marilyn. *History of the Breast.* New York: Ballantine Books, 1998.

____ *How the French Invented Love: Nine Hundred Years of Passion and Romance.* New York: HarperCollins Publishers, 2012.

Yerushalmi, Yosef Hayim. *Zakhor: Jewish History and Jewish Memory.* Seattle: University of Washington Press, 1982.

Young, Brigham. "Beneficial Effects of Polygamy: Remarks by President Brigham Young," *Journal of Discourses* 11 (1866): 266–72.

____ "Gathering the Poor – Religion a Science". *Journal of Discourses* 13 (1871): 300–9.

Zervos, George T. "Seeking the Source for the Marian Myth: Have We Found the Missing Link?" Pages 107–120 in *Which Mary? The Marys of Early Christian Tradition.* Edited by Stanley Jones. *Society of Biblical Literature Symposium Series* 19. Atlanta: Society of Biblical Literature, 2002.

ONLINE PUBLICATIONS

Bumiller, Elisabeth. "Affronted by Nude 'Last Supper,' Giuliani Calls for Decency Panel." New York Times. 2001;

http://www.nytimes.com/2001/02/16/nyregion/affronted-by-nude-last-supper-giuliani-calls-for-decency-panel.html

Chilton, Bruce. "Unmasking a False Gospel." *The Sun*. 2006; http://www.nysun.com/arts/unmasking-a-false-gospel/42197/

Colen, B. D. "Suggestion of a married Jesus." *Harvard Gazette*. 2012; http://news.harvard.edu/gazette/story/2012/09/suggestion-of-a-married-jesus/

Goodacre, Mark. "Jesus' Wife Fragment: Further Evidence of Modern Forgery." NT Blog. 2012; http://ntweblog.blogspot.co.uk/2012/10/jesus-wife-fragment-further-evidence-of.html

Goodstein, Laurie. "A Faded Piece of Papyrus Refers to Jesus' Wife." *New York Times*. 2012; http://www.nytimes.com/2012/09/19/us/historian-says-piece-of-papyrus-refers-to-jesus-wife.html

King, Karen L. "Jesus said to them, 'My wife ...': A New Coptic Gospel Papyrus." DRAFT. *Harvard Faculty Research*. 2012; *http://www.hds.harvard.edu/sites/hds.harvard.edu/files/attachments/faculty-research/research-projects/the-gospel-of-jesuss-wife/29865/King_JesusSaidToThem_draft_0920.pdf*

Pullella, Philip. "'Gospel of Jesus' Wife' should stir thought, scholar says." *Reuters*. 2012; http://www.reuters.com/article/2012/09/19/us-religion-jesuswife-idUSBRE88I10520120919

Rader, Dotson. "Elton John." *Parade*. 2010; http://www.parade.com/celebrity/2010/02/elton-john.html

Raushenbush, Paul Brandeis. "President Jimmy Carter Authors New Bible Book, Answers Hard Biblical Questions." *Huffington Post*. 2012; http://www.huffingtonpost.com/2012/03/19/president-jimmy-carter-bible-book_n_1349570.html

Toufexis, Anastasia. "The Right Chemistry." *Time*. 2001; http://www.time.com/time/magazine/article/0,9171,161030,00.html

Watson, Francis. "The Gospel of Jesus' Wife: How a fake Gospel-Fragment was composed." *NT Blog*. 2012; http://markgoodacre.org/Watson.pdf

REFERENCES INDEX

Biblical Books (Protestant Canon)

Genesis
1:28   152, 189
2:7   45, 173
3   186

Exodus 20:12   119, 127, 159, 184

Deuteronomy   100, 123
7:3   180
23:1   184
28:4–6   187

Ezra   100–104
9–10   101, 180
9:12   101, 180
10:2–3   101, 180
10:10–15   101, 180
10:44   101, 180

Psalm 45   76

Proverbs   16
5   20
5:18–19   16, 168
26:5   83

Ecclesiastes 2:14   83

Song of Songs   93, 99, 137–138
2:4   138, 187
5:2   137, 187
5:3–6   137, 187

Isaiah   74
6:1   74, 176
25:6   187
54:4–6   187
61:10   187

Jeremiah
2:2   187
29:4–7   180–181

Ezekiel 16:8–16   187

Hosea   160
9:11   159, 190
9:14   159, 190

Joel 2:19   187

Matthew   25, 30, 33, 114, 122,
   141, 159
3:7–9   189
5:27–28   185
5:31–32   185
6:25   127, 186
8:14   31, 170
8:17   31
8:19–22   126, 186
8:21–22   158, 189
10:9–10   188
10:34–36   125, 185
10:35–36   189
12:46–50   125, 185
16:28   132, 186
19   140
19:1–12   185
19:10–12   122, 184
19:12   122, 161, 190
19:27   184, 190
22:30   190

Mark   25, 30, 33, 36, 114, 159
1:24   190
1:30   170
2:20   76, 176

3:21   159, 190
3:32–34   158, 190
5:7   190
6:3   29, 170
10:1–12   185
10:17–27   186
11:28–30   1
12:25   190
15:40–41   171
18:20   133, 186

Luke   3, 25, 30, 33, 36, 114,
   126, 150, 157, 159, 160
2:40   115, 183
2:48–49   158, 189
3:7–8   189
3:7–14   186
3:22–24   182
3:23   157, 189
4:38   170
7   54
7:33–34   3, 167
7:37–39   48
8:3   36, 171
8:21   186
11:27   159, 190
11:27–28   126, 150, 186, 189
11:28   159, 190
14:26   125, 158, 185, 189
16:13   185
16:18   185
18:28   124, 161, 184, 190
20:34–36   160, 190
20:35   160, 190

John   9, 25, 54, 74, 114, 159
1:14   9
2:1–11   187
2:4   158, 190
3:39   76, 176
4:7–22   174
8:41   183
10:30   73
19:26–27   190
20:22   45, 173

Acts 2:44–46   188

Letters to the Corinthians   17, 30, 141

1 Corinthians
7:10–11   185
7:29–30   118
9:5   31, 170

2 Corinthians
8   139, 188
8:14   188
11:2   139, 188

Philippians 4:3   170

Letters to Timothy   17

1 Timothy 3:4–5   184

Revelation   135, 187
3   138
3:20   137, 187
19   138
19:7   136, 187
19:7–8   138, 187
19:9   138, 187

Extracanonical Gospels

Gospel of the Egyptians   34–36, 41

Gospel of Mary   47, 49

Gospel of Philip   41–49, 57,
    66, 163, 173
11–12   43, 172
31   43, 46, 173
59   42, 172
99   173

Gospel of Thomas   3, 25, 33,
    35, 36, 41, 45, 49, 150
47   185
55   185
61   35, 171
79   150, 158, 186, 189–190
86   186
108   45, 173
114   173

Proto-Gospel of James   33–36,
    150–151, 171
19   150, 189
19:3–20:1   34, 170

Secret Mark   see *Letter to Theodore*

Other Christian Writings

Anonymous, *The Lady Poverty*   188
Augustine, *On Marriage and
Concupiscence*
1.4   20, 169
1.5   20, 169

Clement of Alexandria,
   Stromateis
3.7   169
3.45   35, 170
3.49   22, 169, 139, 188
3.53   170
3.59   21, 169
3.74   141, 188

Gregory I, *Homiliarum in
   evangelia* 33   54, 174

Irenaeus, *Against
Heresies* 1.28   139, 188

Jerome, *On Marriage and
   Virginity* 22.19   19, 169

Origin, *Against Celsus* 3.10   177

Shepherd of Hermas 11   18–19

Thomas Aquinas, *Summa
   Thaeologica* 153.2   20, 169

Greek and Roman Writings

Galen, *Commentary on
   Plato's Republic*   17, 168

Homer, *Hymn to Apollo* 3   187
Rufus, *Discourses* 13b   181

Tacitus, *Annals* 3.25   184

Dead Sea Scrolls

1QSa 1:9–11   110, 182
War Scroll 7:1–2   189

Rabbinic Writings

m. Aboth 5.21   155, 189
m. Nid. 5.4   182
m. Yeb. 10.18   182
b. Qidd. 29b–30a   108, 182
b. Yeb. 10.9g   113, 183
b. Yeb. 62b   106
Mosseri (Cairo Geniza)
   7.68.A   152, 189

Persian Poetry

Layla and Majnun   94
Masari al-Ushshaq   94

Chinese Poetry

Fu Xüan, *Woman*   27

Disputed Writings (Relative
to Modern Forgery Claims)

"Celsus" in Mormon Writing   77

Gospel of Jesus' Wife   62–67

Letter to Theodore
I.10   83
I.20–21   83
II.2–10   84

SUBJECT INDEX

Allison, Dale C.   146, 186

Anderson, Janice Capel   128, 185

Apollonius of Tyana   189

Apostolic church   23, 41, 43

Aquinas, Thomas   20, 169

Asceticism   2, 4, 14–21, 23, 128, 131, 162

Atkinson, Kenneth   170

Augustine of Hippo   20–21, 24, 169

Augustus (Caesar)   121, 154

Aune, David   146, 187

Babatha   111–112, 183

Bagley, Will   177

Baigent, Michael   175

Bancroft, J. H. J.   182

Bauckham, Richard   170, 171

Baumgarten, Albert   82, 178

Bell, Joseph N.   105, 180

Bennett, John C.   75

Bernhard, Andrew   64–65, 175

Big Lebowski, The   11, 19, 169

Blenkinsopp, Joseph   105

Blickenstaff, Marianne   146, 184, 187

Bloch, R. Howard   180

Blum, Edward J.   175

Boer, Esther A. de   68

Bogin, Magda   105, 180

Bond, James   10–11, 13, 168

Bored to Death   10

Bowden, John   68

Brakke, David   52

Breasts   15, 126, 149–151, 156, 160, 188–189

Brown, Dan   40, 60, 66, 175

Brown, Peter   24

Browning, D. S.   116

Buonarroti, Michelangelo   70

Burke, Tony   90

Calder III, William M.   178

Calvin and Hobbes   5

Carlson, Stephen C.   89, 178–179

Carter, Jimmy   81

Carveth, Rod   179

Catholic Church   12, 30, 55, 66, 69, 80, 82, 85, 165, 174

Celibacy   2, 9, 12, 15, 17, 108,

109, 111, 121–122, 128, 131,
139–140, 145, 157, 160, 182
Celsus (critic of
Christianity) 77–79
Celsus (medical
philosopher) 77–79
Chapman, Alison 56, 174
Chilton, Bruce 84
Childs, Hal 12, 168
Christianized West 5, 7, 10, 12,
24, 25, 53, 57, 69, 91, 99, 121,
125, 127, 141–142, 162, 163
Civic responsibility 109, 113–114,
124, 128
and masculinity 118–121, 123–124,
125, 127–128, 133–135, 142,
145, 147–148, 157, 160–162
Clare of Assisi 143–145
Clark, Elizabeth 24
Clark, Gillian 18, 173
Clement of Alexandria 22, 32, 34,
82–83, 87, 139, 141–142
Clines, David J. A. 183
Clothing 137–138, 186
Coen, Ethan 170
Coen, Joel 169
Cohick, Lynn 183
Collectivism 99–105, 106, 124–
126, 148, 180
and family 101–105, 109,
113, 118–121, 124–126, 133,
140–141, 142, 145, 152, 159
and fiscal concern 103–104,
113, 118–121, 126–127, 131,
138–139, 142, 144–145
and honor 113–114, 118–121,

126–127, 142, 148, 151–153,
158, 159–161
and patriarchy 104, 106, 109,
120, 124, 126–127, 132,
152–153, 157, 161
Collins, Adela Yarbro 186
Comentale, Edward P. 168
Commemoration 26, 37–38, 41,
51, 55, 57, 119, 125, 130,
148, 165
Conway, Colleen 129, 184
Cooper, Kate 146, 188
Cox, Renée 69–70
Creangă, Ovidiu 129, 183
Cyrus (King) 100

Da Vinci Code, The 40, 60–61, 66,
68, 69, 175
Dafoe, Willem 58, 166
Davies, Douglas J. 90
Dave Matthews Band 59, 91–92
Dead Sea Scrolls 110–111, 189
DeConick, April 41, 44, 52, 168,
171–173
DeMille, Cecil B. 56–57, 91, 174
Derek and the Dominos 94
Donahue, Bill 80
Donne, John 56, 174
Dugard, Martin 186
Dunn, James D. G. 24

Ehrman, Bart D. 39, 43, 68,
172–173, 178
Eliot, George (Mary Anne
Evans) 147
Epictetus 189

Eschatology 132–133, 145, 159–160, 186
Eunuchs 113, 122–124
Evison, E. S. 116
Eyck, Jan van 136

Falsani, Cathleen 167
Feet 54, 187
Ferguson, Sharon 80
Food
    consumption of 3, 35, 142
    abstinence from 2, 15, 17, 133
    as symbol 133–134, 137–138
Foster, Paul 50, 173
Foster, Robert 177
Francis of Assisi 142–145
Francis, James 116
Frost, Robert 101–102

Galen 17, 168
Ganjavi, Nizami 95
Genitalia
    Female 34, 137, 179
    Male 121–122, 187
George, Mark K. 184
Giuliani, Rudolph 69–70
Glancy, Jennifer A. 171
Goodacre, Mark 173–175
Goodstein, Laurie 65
Gospel of Jesus' Wife 62–65, 147, 165
Grant, Jedediah M. 77–80, 176–177
Green, Joel B. 186
Gregory I 54, 56

Haddox, Susan E. 119, 183
Hanson, K. C. 117
Harvey, Paul 175
Historical fiction 3, 33, 34, 37, 42, 55, 57, 61, 148, 150, 164, 165, 174
Hunter, James H. 178
Hurtado, Larry 170

Ilan, Tal 37, 170, 172–174
Imus, Don 177
Individualism 99–101, 103, 180–181
Inheritance 120–121
Irenaeus 139, 188

Jaarsma, Ada S. 179
Jacobs, Sandra 169
Jerome 19, 20, 169
Jesus
    and asceticism 23, 128, 140, 144
    birth of 33–34, 59, 183
    as bridegroom 75, 105, 133, 136–139, 141, 143–145, 163
    and celibacy 22–25, 28–30, 69, 122, 128, 131, 139–141, 145, 151–152, 160–162
    death of 32, 34, 131, 164
    and fiscal security 124–128, 132
    as homosexual 80–82, 85, 147, 178–179
    as illegitimately conceived 114–115
    as insane 159

and Judaism   14, 153–154
as lamb   136
as lover   59, 91, 105
as non-physical   21–23
as party goer   3–4, 35–36, 135
as polygamist   74–78, 89, 147, 163, 165
and power systems   71, 127, 130, 133, 157, 165–166
and race   69–71
resurrection of   33
siblings of   29–31, 38, 115, 125, 165, 170, 171
as a woman   69
worship of   42
John the Baptist   1–2, 8, 128, 133, 157
John, Elton   80–82, 89
John (follower of Jesus)   32
Johnson-Debaufre, Melanie   68
Joseph (father of Jesus)   33–34, 114–116, 170
Judas   51

Kazantzakis, Nikos   57, 59, 66, 105, 164–166, 173, 190
Keith, Chris   168, 170
King, Stephen   59, 175
Kissing   54
as spiritual ritual   42, 45–46, 50–51, 147
King, Karen L.   52, 62, 65, 175
Kuefler, Matthew   117

Land holdings   103, 110, 119
Lapin, Hayim   182

Last Temptation of Christ, The   40, 57, 105, 164–166, 173, 175, 190
Latimer, Hugh   55
Law, William   176–177
Le Donne, Anthony   129, 185–186
Leigh, Richard   175
Lerner, Anne Lapidus   37, 39, 172
Levine, Amy-Jill   39, 184
Lewis, C.S.   97–98, 180, 183
Life stages   116, 155–156
Lincoln, Henry   175
Logan, Alastair   188
Longman III, Tremper   179

Mad Men   92, 179
Mar Saba Monastery   82, 87–88
Marcus, Eric   178
Marlowe, Christopher   178
Marriage   2, 92–98, 100–106, 143, 145
ancient customs   97–99, 102–104, 106–109, 111–112, 141, 151–154
arranged marriage   104, 106–107, 113–115, 151–152, 156–157, 182
and divorce   184–185
and fiscal/land concerns   99, 103, 110, 112, 118–121, 138, 144, 151–152, 183
early marriage   104, 106–110, 112–113, 152, 154–155, 182
ethnic/religious intermarriage   100

as holy   152
and life expectancy   109, 112,
      152–153, 155
as motivated by romance   91, 98
polygamy (plural
      marriage)   72–80, 89, 163
as sinful   22, 139–140, 142, 151
Martin, Dale B.   53, 90, 129, 167,
      173, 178–179, 186
Mary (of Bethany)   55, 58–60, 67
Mary Magdalene
   as courtesan   57, 91
   follower of Jesus   3, 33, 36–37,
      40, 51, 161, 165
   jealousy of   41–42, 46
   as lover   40, 42, 57, 59, 62, 67,
      91
   as prostitute   55, 57–60, 163,
      165
   as repentant sinner   54–56, 58,
      67, 174
   as royalty   55, 67, 163
   scandals about   50, 54–55, 58,
      63, 66, 147–148, 163–166
   as symbol   43, 45, 51, 55, 148
   as wife   53–54, 60–62, 65–67,
      128, 161, 163, 174
Mary (mother of Jesus)   29, 31,
      33–34, 114–116, 125, 126,
      149–150, 153, 159, 165, 170
Matera II, Frank J.   146
Matsys, Quinten   48
Meier, John P.   53, 173, 189
Meyers, Carol   103, 110, 181–182
Middleton, Darren J. N.   68, 175

Mills, Michael   179
Misogyny   11, 19–20, 32, 35–36,
      41, 79, 144, 161–162
Moore, Stephen   128, 185
Morales, Helen   181
Mormonism   72–80, 89, 176
Moxnes, Halvor   184
al-Mulawwah, Qays ibn   94

Nag Hammadi Library   41, 42, 57
News media   5, 58, 65–66, 75, 80,
      84, 130, 166, 176–178, 179
Neyrey, Jerome H.   184
Nudity   69–70, 83

Oakman, Douglas E.   117
O'Reilly, Bill   130

Pagels, Elaine H.   141, 188
Parkin, Tim G.   117, 182
Patronage   3, 36, 41, 120, 127–128,
      133–136, 138–139, 161, 174
Patterson, Veronica   59, 91, 175
Paul (Apostle)   14, 15, 17, 23,
      30–32, 40, 106, 118, 141, 182, 184
Persian Love Poetry   93–95, 180
Peter   30, 32, 49, 124, 161
Peter's wife   29–32
Phipps, William E.   105, 181
Picasso, Pablo   70
Pomeroy, Arthur   117, 182
Portefaix, Lilian   184
Pratt, Orson   74–76
Pratt, Sarah Marinda Bates   74–75, 176
Prothero, Stephen   176

Pruss, Alexander R.   24
Puberty   105, 106, 113, 115, 154
Pullella, Philip   66

al-Qayyim, Ibn   93

Rabbis   107–110, 113, 115, 122,
   152, 154, 182
Race   69–70, 102
Reinhardt, Carl   47
Rijn, Rembrandt van   13, 31
Romance (courtly love)   91–92,
   95–98, 104, 134, 145, 180
Roof, Judith   170
Rougement, Denis de   91
Rousseau, Jean-Jacques   69
Rufus, Gaius Musonius   181

Sallman, Warner   71
Salome (follower of Jesus)   3,
   33–37, 41, 147, 165
Sanders, E. P.   186
al-Sarraj   94
Satlow, Michael L.   117, 182–183
Schaberg, Jane   53, 68
Schrader, Paul   175
Schremer, Adiel   183
Scorsese, Martin   40, 57
Secret Mark   83–89
Sexuality
   in ancient storytelling   14
   asexuality   9–10, 12, 142, 160
   and capitalism   10
   coitus   19, 44, 87, 93, 110,
      136–137, 173, 180

and conquest   10–12, 24
eroticism   19, 35, 50, 70,
   92–94, 98, 136–137, 180, 182
and euphemism   86, 93, 137,
   179, 187
fear of   11–12, 14, 151, 162,
   163–166
and fiscal concern   81, 118,
   121, 123, 128, 138
homosexuality   72, 80–82, 85,
   163, 177
and imagination   53, 58, 66,
   97, 105
norms   13, 53, 69, 74, 77, 80,
   89, 104, 112, 121, 122–123,
   125–126, 141–142,
   158, 161
and persecution   72, 85–90
pleasure of   2, 16, 20, 55, 164
preoccupation with   7, 10, 48,
   50, 97, 136, 163
and religion   12, 15–18, 20–23,
   44–45, 69, 110, 141–142,
   147, 161–162
and Satan   22, 139–140
and sin   9–10, 19, 108, 142, 151
struggles with   58, 108, 164
Skinner, Christopher W.   39
Smith, Joseph   72–80, 89, 176–177
Smith, Morton   82–89, 178
South, James B.   179
Spirituality
   enlightenment   41–43, 46
   and gender   44, 49
   hierarchy   44, 48

spiritual family   50, 125–126, 131–139, 150, 157, 159
Spivak, Chakravorty   169–170
Stoyanov, Yuri   174

Tan, Yak-Hwee   169
Tatian   22, 139, 141
Thompson, Augustine   146
Thoreau, Henry David   25
Triandis, Harry C.   105
Troubadours   95–98, 144–145, 180
Turner, John G.   72, 90, 176

Valantasis, Richard   24, 52
Valentinian theology   43–45, 51, 172
Valentinus   21, 43, 172
VanderKam, James   117
Vincent L. Wimbush   24
Voragine, Jacobus de   55, 58, 61

Wagoner, Richard S. Van   176
Waley, Arthur   168
Watson, Francis   63, 87, 175, 178
Watt, Stephen   168
Watterson, Bill   5, 167
Wedderburn, Alexander J. M.   188
Weiner, Matthew   179

Whitmarsh, Tim   181
Wildish, Mark   177
Willman, Skip   168
Women
   as to be avoided   2, 16, 108, 124
   disciples   1, 3–4, 32–33, 36, 147, 173
   and fiscal concern   27, 41, 56, 110, 112, 118–121, 124, 143, 185
   as idealized   55, 59, 95–97, 143–144, 152, 188
   obscured   26–28, 30–32, 33–34, 38, 41, 165
   and poetry   94–98
   and sin   9, 37, 54, 138
   and worship   43
Xenophobia   111
Xüan, Fu   27–28

Yadin, Yigael   111
Yalom, Marilyn   97, 105, 180, 188–189
Yerushalmi, Yosef Hayim   6, 167
Young, Brigham   72–77, 176

Zervos, George T.   172